The Hidden World
of the Pastor

The Hidden World of the Pastor

Case Studies on Personal Issues
of Real Pastors

Kenneth L. Swetland

Baker Books

A Division of Baker Book House Co
Grand Rapids, Michigan 49516

Published by Baker Books
a division of Baker Book House Company
P.O. Box 6287, Grand Rapids, MI 49516-6287

Printed in the United States of America

Library of Congress Cataloging-in-Publication Data

Swetland, Kenneth L.
    The hidden world of the pastor : case studies on personal issues
of real pastors / Kenneth L. Swetland.
      p. cm.
    Includes bibliographical references (p.).
    ISBN 0-8010-9003-2
    1. Clergy—United States—Case studies. I. Title.
BR526.S945 1995
253'.2—dc20   94–49581

To
Anne
with love and gratitude

Contents

Contents

Acknowledgments

I am grateful to the students at Gordon-Conwell Theological Seminary who have used these cases and have given me helpful information in how the cases can be improved. Colleagues at Gordon-Conwell and at other institutions have encouraged me to publish the cases for wider use, and I am grateful for this support. A special word of thanks is due to Scott Gibson, a friend and colleague at Gordon-Conwell, for his good work in helping to compile the bibliography.

My wife, Anne, and sons, Brock and Reid, as well as good colleagues along the way have been used by God to teach me things about myself that I needed to know. I am better for it. And I am still learning. My thanks to them for their help.

Introduction

*T*here is no question that pastors are under great stress today. This is not a new phenomenon, of course, since ministry has always brought with it difficulties. Sometimes these are of the pastor's own doing. Sometimes they are caused by people whom the pastor serves. Sometimes they reflect the activity of the evil one. Although the Christian's hope is always that righteousness will triumph in the coming age because of the victory over sin and evil won by Christ on the cross, difficulties do exist today. They tear at the heart of the pastor but are often hidden from the view of the congregation.

A pastor I know recently told me, "Never has there been a time when congregations expect so much of their pastor and so little of themselves." Lay people do expect a great deal of their pastors today, but pastors also expect a great deal from themselves. Add to this the tendency for pastors to be "lone rangers" with few significant people to talk to apart from their spouses if they are married, and we have an atmosphere ripe for disappointment, conflict, and failure.

We who are leaders in the church need to be talking to each other about the issues of our lives. No one understands ministry better than we who are involved in it day to day, so we are in the best position to understand, encourage, and challenge each other. But often this is the very thing we are reluctant to do. We who help others often bury our own burdens within our souls.

Of course, finding support in friends and colleagues is no substitute for the inner strength that comes from a growing and healthy relationship with God. He is indeed the "friend who sticks closer than a brother" (Prov. 18:24). Nor is companionship with others a substitute for good theology, which understands biblical teaching and applies this teaching to one's own life. Nor should we disregard Paul's advice to the Galatian believers: "Each one should carry his own load" (6:5). But in the preceding phrases Paul also challenged these Christians to "carry each other's burdens, and in this way you will fulfill the law of Christ" (6:2). The "burden" of verse 2 is the crushing weight that is too much for one person to bear, and the "load" of verse 5 is the "backpack" each Christian should carry on his or her own. It takes wisdom to know the difference between the two, but that wisdom is the very quality that can make a big difference in how we do ministry and how we grow spiritually in our relationship with Christ.

In this book my primary concern is for those who are trying to carry alone a burden that God wants our friends to share, the friends whom he has given in his wisdom and providence. Ministers sometimes fail because they would rather go it alone than seek counsel from someone else. We would rather be the helper than the helpee, and while this is not bad in itself, it becomes debilitating when our ministry flounders because we are not paying attention to matters that need to be addressed in our own lives.

The pastor who has a "soul friend" is indeed blessed. It does not take a large group to provide such support. Even one or two people can provide good perspective for us. God has redeemed us as individuals, but he has also placed us in community. We pastors are far better at helping others find this community than we are at finding it ourselves. And we are weaker for it.

The cases presented in this book are intended to be used by students and pastors in small discussion groups. Cases provide an opportunity for pastors to look at their own hidden world by discussing the issues presented in the stories. Pastors best understand the pastoral world and are the best human resource for support, correction, accountability, and encouragement to one another. Our competitiveness and isolation can prevent us from doing this, however. Therefore let me encourage pastors and students studying to be pastors to use this case book in discussion groups as a way not only of stretching the intellectual muscles as various issues are debated with colleagues, but also of helping individuals examine their own hidden world and deal with personal issues.

The goal of this endeavor is not to encourage pastors and students to be more preoccupied with the inner self—a preoccupation that has run amok in our culture—but to know oneself better in order to minister to others better. The goal is not to be psychologically whole, although that is an important by-product, but to be spiritually whole and passionately obedient to God. Sometimes our problems get in the way of doing this freely.

John 13:1 says, "Jesus *knew* that the time had come for him to leave this world and go to the Father. Having loved his own who were in the world, he now showed them the full extent of his love" (italics added). In verses 3–5 John says, "Jesus *knew* that the Father had put all things under his power, and that he had come from God and was returning to God; so he got up from the meal, took off his outer clothing, and wrapped a towel around his waist. After that, he poured water into a basin and began to wash his disciples' feet" (italics added). Jesus' obedience to the Father in ministering to the disciples is directly connected to his *knowledge* of who he was. So when he noted that the disci-

13

ples called him "Teacher" and "Lord" (v. 13), he commanded that they also wash each other's feet as a symbol of humble and obedient service (v. 14). "I have set you an example that you should do as I have done for you," he said (v. 15). Our ability to serve competently and obediently as pastors is enhanced when we know who we are, who God is, and what he has called us to do. Only in this sense is self-knowledge crucial. A careful reading and discussion of the cases in this book can aid such self-knowledge.

All of the cases are true stories based on my interviews over the last three years of a variety of pastors from different parts of the country, from different denominations, of different ages, and from different backgrounds. Some of the pastors volunteered to be interviewed when they heard about the project. Others were contacted by me because I thought their stories would benefit other pastors. All have consented willingly to have their stories told. Most indicated they hoped others would benefit from their experience. Thus, telling the story had a redemptive effect for many of the pastors. For several, just telling the story to me liberated them to move forward in dealing with issues that had been either hidden or ignored by them up to this point.

A common thread through many (not all) of the interviews is that pastors who experience difficulty sometimes have not adequately dealt with issues in their background. Although my role in conducting the interviews was that of a reporter getting information, I occasionally became more of a counselor and friend in reflecting with the person on what had happened. Many of the pastors said I was the only person to whom they had ever told the story. This speaks of the need for pastors to cultivate friendships with other pastors who can offer knowledgeable support and counsel in a way no one else can. Such people can provide both affirmation and helpful criticism when needed. Too many pastors settle for cordiality with other ministers when collegiality is what is needed.

While the core of information in every case is true, certain identifying elements have been disguised. Individual names, places, names of churches, and areas of the country have all been changed to protect privacy. In a few cases the pastor's denomination has been changed as well, but only to a compatible group so the issues make sense in a given context. Such disguising of information is common and recommended practice in case writing.

When I have used these cases, occasionally someone will approach me to say they know who the person in the case is. Invariably they are wrong, but it illustrates the commonality of the issues. More often than not, someone in the group will say that this could just as well have been their story. Indeed, these stories are our stories.

In typical case style, the stories end without resolution. (Some of the cases had happy endings, some not so happy, and others are still evolving.) Unknown endings allow readers to grapple with the issues and learn from the stories. So bring resolution to the case yourself, using biblical understanding, theological thinking, and your knowledge of human nature.

A variety of issues are reflected in the cases: anger, depression, guilt, money problems, family difficulty, call to ministry, candidating, marital stress, sexual infidelity, divorce and remarriage, congregational conflict, staff relationships, and spirituality, among others. Different groups will identify different issues for discussion. Some issues are readily apparent, others more subtle.

While the cases are intended for group discussion, individuals can benefit from reading the cases and examining their own lives. Personal questions can be asked and ideas can emerge that will help individuals be more mature and godly in their own work. The audience I envision for the book is clergy, but lay people could also benefit from reading and discussing the cases as a way of understanding the world of pastoring and of offering reasoned support and godly counsel to their own pastors.

To allow the readers to develop the discussion as desired, teaching notes for the cases are not provided. Suggestions for how to teach cases in general are noted in the appendix. For those who want to read about particular issues presented in the cases, a bibliography is provided at the end of the book.

All the cases reflect some sort of problem. While many wonderful things are happening in countless churches under capable pastors, in far too many places problems go without attention, debilitating what could be effective ministries. So, taking a problem-oriented approach is a means of learning from other people's struggles so we don't have to repeat their experience.

By confronting problems head-on, we can identify within ourselves issues that need attention for our good, for the benefit of people whom we serve, and for God's glory. A sign hanging over the autopsy room of the general hospital where I did my clinical pastoral education thirty years ago said, THE DEAD TEACH THE LIVING. Although I do not see pastors or the church as dead, good learning can come from negative experience.

Peter wrote to Christians in his day (2 Peter 1:5–8) that they should "make every effort" to develop faith, goodness, knowledge, self-control, perseverance, godliness, brotherly kindness, and love. By possessing these qualities in ever-increasing measure, the believer will be kept "from being ineffective and unproductive in [the] knowledge of our Lord Jesus Christ." Those who do not have these qualities he called "nearsighted and blind." They had forgotten about cleansing from sin.

We pastors do know about sin—our own and others'. Our desire is to be effective and productive, not in the way a pagan culture defines success, but in the knowledge of our Lord Jesus Christ. Knowing ourselves and dealing with issues we need to deal with can contribute to our passionate pursuit of this knowledge of Christ. We are called by him, we serve him in the world, and we will give account of ourselves before him in the coming day.

Thirty years ago when I began pastoral ministry, I was influenced by these words from Richard Baxter in *The Reformed Pastor*:

It is a palpable error in those ministers that make such a disproportion between their preaching and their living that they will study hard to preach exactly, and study little or not at all to live exactly. They are loath to misplace a word in their sermons, or to be guilty of any notable infirmity . . . , but they make nothing of misplacing affections, words and actions in the course of their lives. O how curiously have I heard some men preach; and how carelessly have I seen them live! . . . A practical doctrine must be practically preached. We must study as hard how to live well, as how to preach well. O brethren! It is easier to chide at sin than to overcome it.

I remain challenged by these words. Baxter is right. It *is* easier to chide at sin than to overcome it. Let us work as hard at *living* the Christian life as we do in *preaching* about it. Our goal is greater knowledge of Christ and greater passion and obedience in serving him.

Paul wrote the Corinthians that his suffering flowed from Christ's suffering, and out of that suffering the Corinthians benefited by hearing the gospel of salvation in Jesus Christ (2 Cor. 1:3–7). May the God "who comforts us in all our troubles" help us to come alongside (the root idea of "comfort") others who suffer so they may know the compassion and salvation of the Triune God. To this end the cases in this book are offered.

1

Should Pete Be Reinstated?

Depression/Sexual Sin

*P*ete sat in the outer office of the presbytery building, apprehensive about what the committee in the next room would decide. It had been two years since his divorce and three years since he had left his wife after having had an affair. The church he had served as pastor had dismissed him.

During the past three years he had lived on the street, held menial jobs, been depressed to the point of suicide, and married the woman with whom he had had the affair. Still, he felt a call from God to be a minister of the gospel, and he wanted to continue in the Presbyterian Church USA.

Having completed the three year probationary period, he was now awaiting the final decision of the committee formed by the presbytery to monitor his probation. He did not know what he would do if the committee decided not to reinstate him. "I have experienced the heights and depths of sin and forgiveness," he had told the committee. "I ask you now to forgive me and restore me to the ordained ministry."

As he waited for their decision, his mind flitted over the past: the events of the last three years, his first marriage, his conversion experience, and his original call to ministry.

Pete had grown up in the Presbyterian church. He was baptized when he was four months old, attended services with his parents throughout his childhood, and was active in the youth group as a teenager. "I did all the things church kids were expected to do," he said. When he went to college a few hours away from his home, he found a Presbyterian church where he enjoyed the people and the worship service, and he attended regularly.

Toward the end of his college days, Pete had started to date Barbara, the sister of one of his best friends. Although they had known each other in high school, they had never liked each other. Now that they were dating, friends teased them about what an unlikely couple they were. But the relationship deepened, and three months after Pete graduated from college, he and Barbara were married.

Pete landed a job working for a newspaper, and three months later received his draft notice from the army. The Vietnam War was at its height, and Pete entered the infantry, sure that he would soon be in Vietnam. Out of two hundred people in his unit, only he and one other man were college graduates, so Pete was quickly thrust into a leadership position. The officers in charge of his outfit urged him to go to officer candidate school, but Pete declined. Wanting to end his stint in the army and return to his newspaper job as quickly as possible, he volunteered instead to go to Vietnam. He assumed he would go there anyway, and he thought volunteering might shorten his tour of duty, as had happened with some of his friends. The army, however, sent him to Germany.

Barbara had been able to visit Pete several times while he was in training in the States, and she became pregnant during one of those visits. She joined him in Germany after a few months, and their first child, a girl, was born there.

While stationed in Germany, Pete and Barbara attended chapel services on the army base. Pete observed that the chaplain's duties appeared easier than what he was doing in the infantry, and since he enjoyed religious activities anyway, he applied for a change of status. He received permission to become a chaplain's assistant. In this job he did clerical work and helped with administrative duties but performed no pastoral functions. Still, it was a job he enjoyed, and he felt he was supporting a good thing.

Barbara had gone home after the birth of their daughter to be near her family. Pete missed being with her and their little girl, but he was also a little relieved since there was often tension between him and Barbara.

In Germany Pete encountered a man carrying a cross across Europe, preaching that people should repent and believe in Jesus Christ in a personal way. This hit Pete strongly. His faith had been largely intellectual. He occasionally had wondered about the adequacy of his faith. So he responded to the man's message and believed in Christ. He wrote to his family about his newfound faith, saying, "I have accepted Christ as my Savior in a personal way, and I'm very excited about it." They called to express concern that he would become "a religious fanatic." He responded that his experience was real and they needed to embrace the Christian faith in a personal way, too.

Barbara returned to Germany, and before long she accepted his challenge and also committed her life to Christ. Together they began a new journey of faith. Pete read everything he could get his hands on about Christianity, and he and Barbara were involved in Bible studies that excited them.

When Pete was discharged from the army, he and Barbara returned to their home in the States. Pete got his job back as a newspaper reporter and writer, and was also involved in a restaurant he had invested in earlier, a business which was going well. He and Barbara quickly got involved in a local Presbyterian church, a different one from the one he had attended as a child. Soon he was teaching a Sunday school class, leading a weeknight Bible study for adults, and participating in the church's Evangelism Explosion program. He was also involved in a weekly prayer breakfast for men through the local Christian Businessmen's Committee. Within a year after joining the church, Pete was made a deacon and later the moderator of the board of thirty-three people.

By this time Pete and Barbara had a second child, a son. Pete was busy with church involvement, his newspaper work, and the restaurant business. They bought a house with over an acre of land, which demanded a great deal of upkeep. "To say I was busy was putting it mildly," said Pete. But he enjoyed it all and felt immensely happy with his life—except for his marriage.

When Pete married Barbara, he knew that the two of them had very different outlooks on life and approached tasks with very different styles. But he also knew that was part of what he found attractive in Barbara. He approached life head-on and tackled tasks with enthusiasm, seeing things through from beginning to ending. Barbara, on the other hand, was artistic and creative and would seldom finish a task she started. Even though she did not work outside the home, Pete did much of the housework and cooking, since he liked the house to be neat and the meals to be well-prepared. The tension that had been present almost from the beginning between Pete and Barbara now broke out in frequent fights. They did not know how to communicate or fight fairly.

During one particularly intense exchange, Pete feared they were about to hit each other or throw something at each other. He requested they get professional counseling, but she refused. Later when they had both calmed down, he again requested—begged might be a better word—that they get counseling, but she again declined. The more he asked her to go to a counselor with him, the more adamantly she refused, saying that going to a counselor was an admission of failure and she did not think they had failed.

Despite the tension in his marriage, things were going well for Pete in his church work, and he began to sense a call to pastoral ministry. In a way this surprised him since he enjoyed his lay ministry and his businesses. He tried to forget what he felt, finding the whole thing a bit frightening, but the sense of call persisted. So he made an appointment to discuss it with his pastor. "I think the Lord may be calling me to be a pastor and to go to seminary to prepare for this ministry," he told the pastor.

"If that's true," the pastor replied, "you'll never be happy doing anything else."

When Pete told Barbara, to his surprise she said, "Let's do it!" That was the confirmation he needed.

Pete visited a nearby seminary, thinking he could commute to classes and continue with his restaurant business. But his visit was disappointing. Pete was turned off by the profane language of an admissions counselor and angered by graffiti on the walls of several buildings at the school. When Pete asked the admissions counselor what he would learn about the Christian faith at the school and the counselor replied, "We don't deal with faith here," that was the final straw.

When Pete told his pastor about the seminary visit, his pastor urged him to look elsewhere. He recommended another school, and Pete made arrangements to visit, even though it was more than a day's drive from home and was not affiliated with his denomination. When he talked with the admissions counselor at this seminary, he found him to be a man filled with "sweetness, faith, and love," and he fell in love with the school.

Barbara rejoiced with him, and together they prepared to go away to school. By this time a third child, another girl, was born to Pete and Barbara, so going to seminary was no minor undertaking. But their house sold quickly and for a good profit. Pete was also able to sell his interest in the restaurant, so they had enough money to finance seminary studies without either of them having to work.

Pete and Barbara had been Christians three years when they went to seminary. Both were twenty-nine years old, and they looked forward to what they thought would be like a three-year Bible study. Pete felt quickly intimidated, however, by the rigorous academic program and the high caliber of the other students. For the first six weeks he was miserable and thought he had made the biggest mistake of his life. He was scared and felt stupid as he compared himself to other students. But Pete and Barbara made friends and began to see that he could handle the coursework. They felt more comfortable, and life settled into a good routine.

While at seminary Pete developed close friendships with five other married male students. Together they laughed and studied and prayed their way through seminary. It was a good time, and Pete felt confirmed in his call to ministry. His field education brought him face-to-face with a wide range of pastoral tasks—all of which he enjoyed—and he received affirming comments wherever he ministered. Pete finished seminary in three years and went on to complete a Th.M. at a Presbyterian seminary.

In seminary the tensions that had existed all along between Pete and Barbara continued, but his enjoyment of the studies, the good camaraderie with his friends, and the exciting church ministry he was in took his mind off his marriage troubles.

After Pete finished the Th.M., he was called by a PCUSA church to be the pastor. The congregation numbered 110 and was composed mostly of blue-collar workers. The real world of ministry hit Pete immediately. In his first week at the church, he dealt with the rape of a parishioner and a suicide, and he conducted a funeral. In the months that followed, his counseling load was heavy, but he enjoyed the ministry and was grateful to God for the growth that was occurring in the church. Pete worked long hours and was exhausted much of the time. But he came home from the office each day and did the laundry, cooked supper, cleaned the house, and put the three children to bed. Barbara still did not work outside the home, but she seldom did anything to make the house livable. She began projects such as washing or ironing but would leave them undone, and Pete would have to finish them when he got home.

It seemed to Pete that Barbara was becoming more disorganized all the time. Even though he would tidy up the manse one day, the next day things would again be in disarray. He frequently asked Barbara to try harder, and he requested that she talk with someone who could help her develop organizational skills, but she refused. She loved her artistic outlets and spent most of each day on her projects or reading. Pete wanted the manse to look good since they had frequent visitors who came to the house for counsel or assistance, but it was up to him alone to keep things organized and neat—a reality he was increasingly resenting.

Pete often wondered why Barbara never finished anything. She had never received her college degree even though she had plenty of credits, but had switched majors so many times that she was never able to form a concentration in any one subject to allow her to graduate. Even many of her artistic projects or crafts were never completed, but sat around the house in various stages of development. But Pete felt helpless to do anything about it. When he tried to talk with Barbara about it, she would become upset and a loud argument usually followed.

After four years at this church, during which time the congregation had grown to 170 people, Pete was called to his second church.

This church was composed mostly of professional people. They loved to deal with ideas, and Pete felt there was a good match between his interests and the people's. Even though Pete had seen good growth in his first church—both in numbers and in his ability to pastor the people—he had always referred to himself when with other ministers as the "unintentional interim pastor." This was partly because Pete had followed a minister who had been at the church for twenty-seven years, but was also because Pete felt he was not the right person for the needs of the people.

Pete was very happy in his second church, and the ministry was going well, but he continued to be unhappy with his marriage. He knew Barbara was unhappy, too. He now saw her as a chronic complainer who was never satisfied with anything and never thought anything he did was worthwhile. He had tried through the years to give her emotional support, but he never felt she supported him the same way. Now he stopped giving her any kind of support.

The church had a creative ministry to the community and was growing in numbers. Pete was well liked by the congregation and popular in the community. A few people sensed that all was not well between Pete and Barbara, but no one knew the tension was so great that Pete was avoiding going home. Were it not for the children and his desire to be with them, Pete knew he would seldom be at home. When he was in the house, he sometimes had to leave for a few minutes to calm his own emotions and lower the tension.

Soon after they had arrived at the church, Pete and Barbara made good friends with another couple, Don and Janie. Their oldest daughter had become a friend with one of Don and Janie's daughters, and the families frequently got together for cookouts, restaurant dinners, and social activities. Both Don and Janie were active in church, Don as an elder and Janie as a Sunday school teacher. Pete had observed occasionally some tension between Don and Janie, but on the whole their relationship seemed stable, and Pete greatly enjoyed the time the two families spent together. Don was, in fact, his best friend.

One day Janie came to see Pete at the church office to talk about stress in her marriage. She revealed Don was occasionally abusive with her, and she had reason to believe he was unfaithful. She said the problems were long-standing, that she had been to several counselors, but that there had been no change in her relationship with Don. For his part, Don had refused to go to a counselor with her.

Pete told Janie that because of the friendship between their two families, he did not think he was the best one to offer her counsel. He also knew he found her very attractive and did not want to be tempted by being alone with her. So he referred her to another pastor.

A few weeks later Pete went to Don and Janie's house to help them move to a new place. While carrying a box out of a room, he noticed Janie look at him in a romantic way. *Oh, no!* he thought. *This is scary.* He knew he felt something for her, but he did not want to pursue it. That night he called his executive presbyter and revealed he might be falling in love with one of his parishioners and he felt vulnerable since his own marriage was shaky.

"Well, work it through," the man responded. "You know what to do." Pete did not tell the presbyter that, in fact, he did not know what to do.

Don and Janie invited Pete and Barbara over for dinner a few days after settling into their new home. Pete sensed that he shouldn't go because the thought of seeing Janie was too exciting. Pete often hugged his parishioners and would kiss women on the cheek (many parishioners had commented on how warm and affectionate he was), but as he and Janie embraced at the door of their home he felt more was being communicated than socially accepted affection. Again he was frightened by his feelings, but he felt helpless to control them.

When the evening came to a close, Pete followed Janie into the bedroom to get their coats, and suddenly he and Janie fell into a passionate embrace and kiss. It lasted only a few seconds, but Pete found it intensely exciting. At the same time he knew he was nearing the point of no return. As he and Barbara drove home in silence (their all-too-familiar silence) he vowed never to do such a thing again.

Pete had often preached against what he saw as the "three worst sins: abortion, homosexuality, and divorce." On more than one occasion he adamantly vowed in public that he would never get divorced. Even as he said the words, he wondered deep down if his words were not just bravado that he hoped would prevent what he feared. Now contradicting in his behavior the very things he had preached so strongly about, Pete felt waves of guilt sweep over him, and he began to wonder if he could continue in the ministry.

Still, Pete called Janie frequently from the office. They talked freely about their bad marriages and their growing feelings of love for each other. Then Pete often arranged for them to meet to talk about church matters. For several weeks they took long drives in the country where he would park the car in a remote spot, and they would passionately kiss and embrace. Pete fell into a vicious cycle: First he would excitedly plan his next rendezvous with Janie; then he suffered overwhelming feelings of remorse and guilt.

Several times Pete called his executive presbyter and asked for help. Once he told the presbyter he was thinking of leaving the church to deal with his problem. The presbyter encouraged him to stay in the church and work it through since the church was growing and was a good model of ministry to other churches in the presbytery. But he offered no suggestions for help.

Pete felt increasingly ashamed and alone. He knew he was spinning out of control, but he could not stop himself. In one particularly low moment he called the men he had been close to in seminary to get their advice, but to his dismay each one indicated he was having his own problems and was in no position to help. "You know what you have to do," was the typical response. *Yes,* Pete thought, *I do know what to do, but I'm helpless to do it.* Finally the inevitable happened. Pete's parents lived in a nearby town, and while they were away on vacation Pete took Janie with him to check on his parents' home as they had asked. There Pete and Janie had sexual intercourse. Pete told Janie how delighted he was to be with her, how fantastic sex with her was, and how much love he felt for her. She responded similarly. It was an intense experience for both.

That night back home, Pete felt overwhelmed with guilt to the point of being physically sick. He called one of the elders and said he would be unable to preach on Sunday. Then he called his executive presbyter and begged for help. This time the man dropped everything and came to see Pete. In their conversation, in which Pete told all, he recommended Pete get professional counseling.

Pete accepted this recommendation and contacted a Christian psychologist in a nearby town. During one session Pete talked about how his affair with Janie was affecting him spiritually. He felt he could not preach or pray anymore. "I'm too embarrassed to go to the Lord about this," he said. "How can I ask for his help when I already know what I'm doing is against his will?" Feeling he was in a no-win situation, he seriously contemplated suicide. But his love for his children stopped him.

Pete and Janie would resist seeing each other for days, but then one would call the other, and they would soon be back together again. As often as they could they arranged a time and place to have sex, which would be followed by a cycle of guilt and despair for Pete.

He called the friend he felt closest to from his seminary days and asked if he could come to stay for a few days and talk about his problem. The man agreed, and Pete drove several hours to his house. When Pete told him the full story, the man said, "I simply can't comprehend what you're doing! You of all people know how wrong this is! What do you want me to do about it?"

Pete snapped, "I want help, not a lecture!"

Pete soon learned the man and his wife were having their own troubles. That night after everyone had gone to bed, Pete heard them arguing strongly, so he left quietly in the middle of the night and drove home. He realized he was going to have to handle his problem himself. On the way home he hoped he would fall asleep at the wheel and have an accident. Before he reached home, he decided his only option was to tell the elders what he had done and resign as pastor.

The next morning Pete called the elders and requested an emergency meeting for that evening. He also invited the executive presbyter. In the meeting Pete confessed to the affair without saying who it was with, and offered his resignation. The elders were shocked and did not know what to do. They turned to the executive presbyter, who advised them to tell the congregation everything and accept Pete's resignation. He also encouraged them to support Pete's continuing with counseling.

A meeting of the church was held the next Sunday, and the congregation was told what had happened. The congregation gasped at the news. Many people expressed hurt, disillusionment, and betrayal. A few refused to believe it. Some expressed intense anger at Pete for the shame he had brought to the church. Several people requested that the church refuse to accept the resignation and instead send Pete to a rehabilitation program. But the overwhelming majority accepted his resignation, effective immediately. They also voted to give Pete's salary to Barbara for six months and to allow her to stay in the manse for that period of time, but no support was to be given to Pete. The next day church officials removed all of Pete's personal belongings from the office and changed the locks on the door. Even though Pete did not disclose whom the affair was with, in a matter of days word was out that it was Janie. Neither Don nor Barbara knew about the affair, but both had become suspicious in recent weeks. When the details became public, Don asked Janie to leave the house. She went to stay with friends until she could get her own place. Pete confessed to Barbara the nature of the affair on the same day he told the elders. She responded with intense anger, told him she never wanted to see him again, and threw all his clothes and books onto the front lawn of the manse, where they were soaked by a heavy rain. She also began proceedings for a legal separation. Pete gathered up his things from the lawn and moved in with his parents.

After Pete had been at his parents' house a few days, they told him they thought it would be better if he left. They were shocked at what he had done and were having trouble accepting it. Having him stay with them might communicate acceptance of what he had done, and they did not feel they could do that. Pete left immediately and lived out of his car for several months. He wandered the streets at all hours of the day and night. A friendly and understanding director at the local YMCA allowed him several times a week to shower, shave, and do his laundry, but otherwise Pete slept in his car or found a safe place on the street to sleep.

When Pete stopped by the house to see his children one day, his youngest daughter, age nine, slammed the door in his face and said, "We don't want to see you anymore!" Pete was crushed and plunged into deep depression. Within a few weeks he lost twenty-five pounds. Although he no longer was seeing Janie and had vowed not to have any contact with her, she was the only one who reached out to him during his time on the streets. She was concerned about his health and well-being and would drive around looking for him. When she found him, she begged him to come to her place

31

for a meal. He would occasionally go with her, but avoided any sexual contact.

People in the church kept clear of Pete. Former good friends turned and walked away if they saw him in a store, or they looked away if they passed him on the street. Barbara was especially hostile. One day when she saw Pete in the grocery store, she threw a jar at him. It missed but hit a shelf nearby and shattered into pieces. Pete ran from the store with Barbara chasing and yelling at him. She jumped on the hood of the car, denting it as he tried to drive away, and then she followed him in her car as he drove off. Had she not been stopped by the police for running a red light, Pete didn't know what she would have done.

Even the ministers Pete had known in the local ministerial association turned their backs on him. He went to see one man he felt particularly close to, but this minister refused to talk to him and gave him an obscene gesture with his finger. Other Presbyterian ministers requested that the presbytery begin proceedings to remove Pete's ordination. Presbytery officials refused to recommend him for placement anywhere else. Pete saw an advertisement in *Christianity Today* from a church seeking a pastor, and he contacted the church. The search committee was interested in interviewing him until he told them about his situation; then they broke off contact. This happened several times in the weeks following his resignation.

As the weather grew cold, Pete became more uncomfortable living on the streets. Janie begged him to come live with her for his health's sake, and he finally consented. The economy of the area was bad, and despite applying at dozens of places Pete had been unable to find work. Since the church had not participated in the unemployment program of the state, unemployment benefits were not available to him. Janie had a good job, however, and was able to support herself and offer help to Pete, which he reluctantly accepted from time to time. Barbara had obtained a legal separation from Pete, and the terms of the settlement required Pete to pay one thousand dollars a month in child support. The only way he could do this was to borrow against his credit cards.

Finally, Pete landed a job selling appliances at a specialty store. Pete was on commission and quickly started making good money. Soon he was the top salesperson. On one occasion, though, when a couple from the church where Pete had been the pastor came to shop for an appliance, they saw Pete and said loudly, "We don't buy refrigerators from adulterers!" and left the store. Other customers witnessed this and quickly moved away from the conversation. One of the other salesmen, a non-Christian, overheard the conversation, came up to Pete, and gave him a big hug. Pete broke down for a few seconds and quietly said, "I feel so ashamed."

Although Pete was doing well as a salesperson, the store was having trouble making a profit because of the local economy. Consequently the store went into bankruptcy a short time after Pete started working there. The owner decided to move the business to another state where the economy was better, and he asked Pete to join in the venture. Pete agreed to go. It would get him out of the area and allow him to begin again.

A few weeks after Pete moved, Janie moved to be near him. They shared a place but did not have sex. Janie had difficulty finding a job, however, and she missed her children, so she moved back to her previous place to look for a new job. Pete and she agreed they would keep in regular contact by phone and letter. In the meantime, the appliance business was off to a slow start in the new location, and the company reluctantly let Pete go.

When Pete was down to his last ten dollars, he stopped on the spur of the moment and entered a church he was passing. The minister was in his office, and Pete begged him for help in finding a job. Even though the minister did not know Pete, he made some phone calls that resulted in Pete's getting a job doing menial work at a hospital. But it was a job, and Pete felt he could make it financially.

Pete started attending a PCUSA church on Sundays. For several weeks he would slip into the service late and leave before the benediction because he did not want to interact with anyone. One Sunday the minister abruptly walked to the rear of the sanctuary during the singing of the final hymn and stopped Pete as he was about to leave. The minister invited Pete into the office to talk, and Pete reluctantly agreed. When they met later that week, Pete told the minister the whole story. A silence followed Pete's disclosure, and then the minister spoke softly. "I believe forgiveness is real. If you've repented, then seek God's forgiveness, and he'll forgive you." Pete began to cry and prayed for the first time in months. He felt loved and accepted—both by God and this minister.

Pete and Janie had maintained contact with each other while they were separated, as they had agreed to do. In one phone conversation they decided they wanted to be with each other for a time to see if their future together was a realistic possibility, if it was something God would bless. So Janie rejoined Pete in the new location. They lived together, and as they had done previously, they agreed not to have sex. They also began to attend the church where Pete had prayed with the minister.

On one Sunday when the church was celebrating communion, Pete told the minister after the service that he had not taken communion since he resigned his church in disgrace. "I am not worthy," he said.

The minister responded, "I guess Jesus' death on the cross took care of everyone's sin but yours." This stung Pete, but he knew in his heart that the man spoke truth. The next time the church celebrated communion, Pete participated for the first time in two years.

By this time Don and Janie had been divorced for some time. Two weeks after their divorce, Don had remarried someone Janie had all along suspected he was having an affair with.

But Barbara had refused to grant a divorce to Pete. Her lawyer advised her to take this position on the grounds that she would get more money for herself and the children if she were legally separated but not divorced. The lawyer told her Pete would probably pay the money during the separation in hopes of not alienating Barbara, but that he might not pay the money after the divorce. Pete had been able to make all the payments required in the separation agreement in spite of the financial hardship it created for him. He also assured Barbara he would continue to pay a fair amount for her and the children if she would grant the divorce. Both agreed there was no possibility of reconciliation, and in their infrequent talks about business matters or the children's affairs, they could barely conceal their hatred for each other. So it was a relief when Barbara finally consented to the divorce on mutually agreeable terms.

After Pete had resigned from the church, it took almost one year before the presbytery acted on a disciplinary procedure. During the ecclesial trial many lies were introduced as evidence. Church members claimed to have seen Pete and Janie together in places where they had never been. Others said they knew of his having affairs with many women, but Pete knew this was not true, and his accusers could present no hard evidence. Some people even accused him of fathering other children, but Pete was able to disprove this quickly with evidence of his having had a vasectomy after the third child was born to him and Barbara. It seemed to Pete that instead of wanting to discipline him and restore him to a place of ministry, the church wanted punishment and revenge.

The result of the trial was to put Pete on probation for a period of three years but not to remove his ordination. His early and repeated requests for help from the presbytery, which had not been given, was a factor in the final decision.

35

And those in charge of the investigation were convinced both that Pete had genuinely repented of his affair with Janie and that Pete and Barbara had a bad marriage in which reconciliation was not possible. The probation began the day he resigned. During the probation period Pete was not to function as a minister in preaching the Word or in officiating at the sacraments of baptism or communion. A committee was appointed to oversee his discipline, but no support, counsel, recommendations for treatment, or resources were made available to him. He was on his own, and it was not clear how he would be held accountable by the committee charged with overseeing his probation.

Two years after Pete resigned from the church in disgrace and one year after the ecclesial trial, Pete and Janie were married in the church they were attending by the minister who had been kind and accepting of Pete. Shortly after the wedding, the church leaders asked Pete to teach a Sunday school class. Their request moved Pete deeply. "It's been two years since anyone asked me to teach the Bible," he said. Humbly and gratefully he agreed to teach the class.

In the year that followed, he and Janie took on more and more responsibilities for ministry in the church. He felt restored to ministry even if it was done more as a lay person than an ordained minister and even if the presbytery decided not to reinstate him to be eligible for a call in the PCUSA. But he also longed to be a pastor again. Teaching the Bible and ministering to and with people were the joys of his life. He and Janie were developing a close and solid marriage. Others saw this and came to them for counsel, saying things like, "We knew you'd understand what we're going through because you've been through it too," or "I need to find forgiveness the way you have."

The other joy of their lives was they both had been reconciled to their children. Even though the children had opted to stay with the other parent in both cases, Pete and Janie were in regular contact with them and were seeing in many ways the bond of love strengthened between them and their children. The children had forgiven them and were moving forward with their own lives. "This is grace, nothing but grace," Pete frequently said.

As the end of the three year probationary period approached, Pete was asked by the presbytery that disciplined him to come to a meeting with the committee overseeing his probation. Even though they had had nothing to do with him during the probationary period, he was eager to meet with them and to submit to their findings. But he was also apprehensive about the outcome.

At the meeting he recounted the events of the past three years. Nothing was left out, just as nothing was left out in his disclosure at the first ecclesial trial. He now told the committee of his continuing repentance and of his desire to serve in the PCUSA again as a minister of a church. In his final statement to the committee before they adjourned to make their decision, he said, "I have experienced the heights and depths of sin and forgiveness. I never dreamed I would do the things I've done. And I've seen the best and the worst of Christians and the church in response to my behavior. But I praise God that I've been forgiven. Now I ask you to forgive me and restore me to ordained ministry."

The door to the room where the committee had met opened. The chairperson approached Pete. *Will I be reinstated?* he wondered.

2

The Pastor's Daughter Is a Rebel

Family Problems of Pastors

David hung up the phone, tears starting down his cheeks. The director of the drug rehabilitation program where his eighteen-year-old daughter, Gail, was a resident had called to say Gail had left the program during the night, and the staff didn't know where she was. It was not the first time Gail had run away from this facility, and David feared the disastrous results of her previous escape would be repeated.

David, age fifty-one, immediately told his wife, Cathy, age forty-seven, about the phone call. Their tears mingled as they embraced and wondered out loud if there would ever be an end to their turmoil. The immediate question, however, was what should be done about Gail's disappearance.

As the associate minister of an eight-hundred-member church in Louisville, David knew the congregation would understand and be supportive in this new crisis, as they had since he first disclosed his daughter's drug addiction a year ago. But he didn't know whether he and Cathy should leave immediately for the drug treatment facility in Memphis to help look for Gail, or let the local authorities handle it.

Memphis was a six-hour drive away, and they were not sure they would be of any help. And Gail was eighteen, a legal adult, so no one could force her to go back to the treatment program if she were found. Gail had been alienated from David and Cathy for years, so they most likely could not influence her.

To further complicate matters, David was scheduled to preach on the coming Sunday in the senior minister's absence, and this was Friday. Something could probably be arranged, but at the moment nothing came to mind. Then, too, they had Michael, their ten-year-old son, to think about. Although he understood the need for the twice-monthly trips to Memphis for family therapy, he had been complaining more about the long drive.

Feeling emotionally drained as they so often had in recent years, David and Cathy wiped their tears and prayed for wisdom. They especially prayed for Gail that no harm would come to her, that God would redeem her life completely, and that she would know of their love for her. They knew they had made some mistakes in raising her, and they knew Gail was convinced they didn't love her.

Gail was the middle child of three. Her sister, June, was two years older, and Michael was eight years younger than Gail. Both June and Michael were seen by their parents and others as normal children. In fact, others often referred to June as "Miss Goody Two-shoes." June and Gail often fought as they were growing up.

When Gail was born, something about her energized Cathy to give Gail all her attention. In fact, she turned against June, her older daughter, and even felt revulsion for June—for reasons unknown to Cathy then and now. June was quiet and compliant, a darling little girl in every way, whereas Gail came into the world kicking and screaming. From birth she was fiercely determined to be her own person. While this confused and even frightened Cathy at the time, she also rose to the challenge of parenting Gail, perhaps because Gail reminded her of her own rebellious past. So Cathy gave most of her attention to Gail and ignored June. Meanwhile David took over the task of parenting June. They never talked about or analyzed this—it was something they did unconsciously.

In the drug rehabilitation program, Gail told her counselor and later her parents that around age fourteen she concluded she must have been Cathy's child by another marriage and that June was David's child by a different marriage. Since she and June were so different and David and Cathy related to each of them with such exclusiveness, surely they could not be the parents of both her and June. She also recalled thinking as a child that she existed outside the family circle. She felt early in life that she could not trust her father to protect her.

When David heard how Gail felt, he recalled two incidents in her childhood. When Gail was five and David was in seminary, she one day came home after her half day in kindergarten and couldn't get in the house. Cathy was at work, and David forgot Gail would be coming home at that hour, so he was in the shower with the house locked. He did not hear Gail knocking at the door.

It was winter, and Gail became cold and frightened as she waited outside the house. She assumed her father was at home since the car was parked in the driveway and concluded he didn't care about her, deliberately leaving her outside in the cold. When David discovered her outside crying, he rationally explained to her what had happened. He wished now that he could go back and do it over again, this time holding her and crying with her when she was afraid.

The other incident happened when Gail was eight. She was playing with some neighborhood dogs who were playfully jumping around her. At one point she fell down, and the dogs jumped on top of her and were barking. She panicked and screamed for David, who was watching from a few feet away, to rescue her. David sensed she was in no danger and felt she needed to conquer her fears and control her emotions, so he told her to get up on her own. She became hysterical. Finally David jerked her up and scolded her for being afraid and irrational.

Gail said later that she felt shame over being so afraid but also hatred towards her father for not protecting her. And she resolved at that point she would never again trust her father or come to him for help. His action confirmed her worst fears: He would not be there when she needed him, so she would have to make it on her own.

In elementary school Gail was in constant trouble with her teachers. She broke rules and frequently challenged authority. Teacher-parent conferences often focused on Gail's emotional outbursts. At one point school officials diagnosed her as having attention deficit disorder.

By the time Gail was in junior high school she was in complete rebellion against her parents' standards and was running with a rebellious group of young people. She had also begun to experiment with alcohol and drugs. At home she would be compliant and outwardly obedient to her parents' wishes, but behind their backs she flagrantly disregarded their values. She resented her older sister for being perfect in their parents' eyes. A pattern of deceit and avoidance of open conflict developed in the home, and an uneasy tension usually prevailed.

To decrease the family stress, David and Cathy decided to put Gail in a boarding school for her high school years. A family trust fund enabled them to do this without straining their finances. Shortly after going away to school against her wishes, Gail called home in tears: "Please, may I move back home?"

Cathy responded, "It's not emotionally safe for me to have you home right now," so Gail stayed in school but felt deeply rejected.

One of her teachers at boarding school introduced her to marijuana and also engaged in sexual intercourse with her. (The teacher was later released from his position but was never formally charged.) During this time Gail grew increasingly despondent and was sent to a psychologist by school officials. Contributing to her despondency was a breakup with her boyfriend back home. She became suicidal and was sent to a psychiatrist for medication.

The doctor prescribed a drug that was frequently successful in treating depression, but in Gail's case it had the opposite effect, making Gail more depressed and suicidal. David and Cathy talked to the psychiatrist about how poorly Gail was doing, but he encouraged them to "lighten up" and said there was nothing wrong with Gail's use of marijuana, cigarettes, and alcohol. "This is just what young people do today," he said.

Gail finally prevailed upon her parents to allow her to return home from boarding school to live with them and attend the local high school. Back with her old friends, Gail began to use stronger drugs. One night David answered the phone and was told by an unidentified male that Gail had taken some drugs and was "on a bad trip," but he hung up before David could find out where Gail was. David went out looking for Gail but couldn't find her. It was the longest night of his life. The next day was Sunday and David was scheduled to preach. Somehow he got through the day, but he never told anyone about what was happening.

Gail came home that Sunday in a stupor from the drugs she had taken the night before and said she had been raped by two of the men in the group she was with. David and Cathy took her to the hospital. After they returned home, they told Gail she was grounded for two weeks. Gail seemed relieved with the discipline but soon rebelled against it. "Trying to discipline Gail is like trying to nail jello to the wall," David would say.

Although she was grounded, Gail obtained some marijuana laced with a potent drug. She took it at home and passed out. It was a holiday, so when David and Cathy found her in a stupor in her bedroom, they did not take her to a hospital, thinking she would sleep it off. They decided to take her to a local addiction-treatment center the next day. The next morning, they told Gail. Gail called a friend who raced up to the house in his car a short time later. Gail ran out of the house, jumped into his car, and they sped away. David ran after them for a short distance and got the license number of the car.

David called the police with the information, and an official search began, since Gail was only seventeen and legally a minor. One week later the police located the car and found Gail in an apartment with a friend.

David and Cathy had heard about a drug rehabilitation center in Memphis and made arrangements to take Gail there whenever the police found her. Immediately upon Gail's return to the house by the police, David and Cathy put her in the car and left for Memphis.

Gail cried all the way from Louisville to Memphis, repeatedly begging her parents not to put her in the program. David and Cathy told her of their love for her and their desire to get help. "We will never give up on you," David said. Although David and Cathy thought Gail needed a highly structured environment to help her control her life, they were also concerned about the harsh discipline they had heard about from friends on the part of the staff of the drug rehabilitation facility. So while they felt confident about the good reputation of the center for helping young people who had not been helped elsewhere, and which had been recommended to them by trusted friends, they did not want anything to happen to Gail there that would hurt her or further alienate her from them.

David and Cathy settled Gail at the treatment center and the next day drove home. They were exhausted. Up to this point they had not told anyone beyond their closest friends about Gail, but on the drive home they decided it was time to tell the congregation. They did not know how people would respond, but they wanted the congregation to be praying. They also wanted people to understand why they might be edgy, tired, or preoccupied on occasion.

David first told the senior pastor. He was shocked and recommended David tell no one, fearing how the congregation might respond. David's job description included counseling, and the pastor feared that people might see David as not running his own household affairs well and so would not come to David for counsel.

David wondered if the senior pastor's own background—he had grown up with an alcoholic parent—had colored his thinking. The pastor had always been uncomfortable telling anyone about what he saw as private business.

In the end David decided to tell the congregation. He informed the pastor, who went along with David's decision, and then the church, and he was pleased with how the people responded. There was a huge outpouring of love and support for David and Cathy. Church members regularly assured them of their prayers and frequently asked how things were going. People also came to David for counsel, saying they knew he would understand their situation since he had been through a difficult time himself. Even the senior pastor started to open up to people in the church about his upbringing and found people also accepted and loved him in spite of what he saw as a shameful experience.

In addition to their prayers and emotional support the church readily gave David time off so the family could go to Memphis two times a month for the family therapy sessions required by the treatment center. David, Cathy, and Michael (June was away at college) found the trips exhausting physically and emotionally, but they were willing to do it to help Gail get better. And they were learning things about family communication.

45

In their talks with the staff at the center, David and Cathy began learning how to talk about feelings. Both David and Cathy grew up in families where life was approached in rational terms only. As a result they had never talked with each other or the three children about feelings. They realized that Gail, who was born with her emotions on the surface, needed to be free to talk about how she felt. Gail had never felt accepted by them because she never felt they understood her or really tried to communicate with her.

With this new insight, they resolved to talk more about feelings within the family, especially since they now realized that Michael appeared to bury his feelings, and they did not want him to experience what Gail had. It was hard work, and they wondered if it might be too late to be reconciled to Gail and have a close relationship with her.

The family sessions encouraged David and Cathy to look back on their own lives and think about anything that might affect their relationship with Gail. Cathy had grown up in a Christian family with a grandfather who was a minister, but she had never embraced the Christian faith as a young person, although her family thought she had. To live her life without scrutiny from her parents, Cathy moved across country to work after college. At work she met David, and they quickly fell in love. David was an agnostic—if not an atheist—at that time, but he also loved to debate religion.

David and Cathy lived together before they got married. At one point after their marriage, David was laid off from work for seven months. This put a strain on their finances and marriage, and David turned to the church for help. His gods were power and money, and when those were gone, he was scared. He sought out a minister to ask questions. David asked one minister to tell him about Jesus, and the man replied, "I really wish I could tell you, but I'm not sure either." So David began attending another church where he thought he could get answers to his questions. At one evangelical, charismatic church he heard about the Christian faith in a logical and coherent way for the first time, and he became a Christian.

Cathy was put off by David's newfound faith. She had initially been attracted to David's spunk and self-confidence, and she feared he would be different after becoming a Christian. To make matters worse for her, he was even talking about becoming a minister. To her the whole thing was humiliating. She did attend church with David, however, but she described it as "quaint and prehistoric." Being serious about religion was not something educated people did, she reasoned.

For a while she attended a Unitarian-Universalist church because she thought their approach to religion made more sense. One Sunday, however, she visited David's church again and felt something happen inside. "I felt the presence of the Lord for the first time," she said, and she, too, soon became a Christian. Not long afterward they left for seminary and a life jointly committed to Christian ministry.

Reflecting on her own background, Cathy knew she and Gail had much in common. Both were born rebels who chafed at authority. Both wanted to control their own lives. David's own reluctance to talk about anything except in the most rational of terms added to the problem.

From the beginning Gail resisted cooperating with the staff and program requirements at the treatment center. She wanted to be with her friends. She wanted to control her own life. She wanted drugs. The staff had diagnosed her as having an addictive personality disorder, a problem very difficult to treat without the addicted person's cooperation.

After being at the program a few months, Gail ran away and hid at a house with some friends who had graduated from the treatment program. Within days she was back on drugs and on one occasion had sex with a stranger.

Several weeks later she experienced internal physical pain and was taken by her friends to the hospital emergency room. The doctor informed her she was pregnant and that she had chlamydia, a sexually transmitted disease. Gail called David and Cathy and told them about her situation, but she would not reveal where she was. She asked for money for an abortion. They refused to send her money because they thought abortion was wrong, and they begged her to return to the treatment facility. They assured her over and over of their love for her and their willingness to help with the pregnancy. Undaunted, Gail turned to Cathy's parents for money. They sent it to her knowing it was for an abortion. They told Cathy and David they thought it was the best thing for Gail under the circumstances.

Meanwhile David had hired a private detective to locate Gail, and he was able to use the phone call from Gail to find her. The authorities picked her up in a ramshackle house in a rural area not far from Memphis and returned her to the treatment facility at the request of David and Cathy. She continued to be uncooperative and vowed to flee again as soon as she had an opportunity. That opportunity came a few months later. Now Gail was gone again. The treatment center had called David and Cathy. And they had no idea what to do.

As Christians in the charismatic tradition, David and Cathy often felt God's presence with them in their daily activities, and they relied upon God's leading. At times each of them had even heard God speak audibly to them giving them direction. But heaven was strangely silent at this moment. Should they go to Memphis? Should they wait at home to hear from the authorities? Or was there some other course to take?

3

Can Dirk Survive?

Staff Relationships

Dirk felt his stomach tighten as he thought about the elders meeting he would be attending that evening. The previous two meetings had done nothing to resolve the conflict between him and Gordon, the senior pastor. In fact, those meetings had made matters worse. Nor was there any progress in the senior minister's personal problems. He and his wife, Virginia, had been charged with fraud by the travel agency where she worked part-time organizing trips to overseas locations and where he acted as tour leader and lecturer on these trips. Most of the people who went on the trips were from the church.

When the accusation of fraud came to the church leaders' attention and was not resolved, Dirk hoped to help bring reconciliation between Gordon and the leaders. But instead, he had become part of the conflict as a result of his attempting to provide leadership when it appeared to him to be lacking in others, including Gordon. And now Gordon was accusing him of disloyalty and of being a busybody. Dirk felt as if he were being made a victim. Rather than feeling as if he were becoming a leader, Dirk felt the past was about to be repeated.

Dirk, who was thirty-five, had pastored two small churches before taking this position as an associate, but he had always seen himself as a weak leader. He often felt inadequate as a pastor, so it did not take much for him to question whether he was doing the right thing. He had never been in a situation as complicated or intense as this and he could not shake the feeling that somehow this was his fault.

He initially accepted this position as an associate because he had looked forward to working with an experienced pastor who was older than he was and who could guide him through the intricacies of church life. He thought he had found this when he first began working with Gordon, who was fifty-eight. But here he was, embroiled in conflict after being at the church less than a year, and he wondered if he would survive.

As he pondered his situation, Dirk looked back on his rather tumultuous Christian pilgrimage. At college Dirk was converted through a campus Christian organization. He had been planning to be a coach and work with young people, but after living in a house with several Christian men for a year, he began to think seriously about Christian ministry. He was beginning to suspect that he was not assertive enough to be a coach. When he raised the question about Christian ministry with his friends, they encouraged him in that direction.

Dirk applied to a seminary on the West Coast. Seminary was a good experience for him as he learned more about the Christian faith and felt confirmed in his call from God to pastor. He felt a special yearning to work in the area of church renewal in a liberal denomination such as the United Church of Christ he had grown up in, and where he had not known about the possibility of personal faith in Christ. One of his seminary professors had influenced him toward missions, and Dirk felt he could happily minister in what he saw as a mission field here in the United States. Since his family still attended a United Church of Christ and he had not become affiliated with any other denomination, he pursued ministerial standing and ordination with the UCC. During his field education in a UCC church, Dirk met Julie, a young woman who attended the church. Julie was from a Roman Catholic background but was not sure she was a Christian. She attended the UCC church because she wanted to know more about the Christian faith. Dirk found her attractive and winsome, and they began dating.

Frequently Dirk and Julie had long talks about the Christian faith. As the relationship developed, he had the privilege of helping Julie embrace the Christian faith fully so that she could say without reservation that she was a Christian. Dirk was thrilled when this happened because he saw her conversion as a confirmation of his call to work for renewal in a liberal setting. He also realized he was falling deeply in love with Julie and she with him. When he graduated from seminary, they were married.

Dirk was called to be the pastor of a two-point charge in the Pacific Northwest. One church was affiliated with the UCC and the other with the American Baptist Churches. Each time there was a pastoral vacancy in the yoked parish, the churches alternated between the UCC and the ABC in selecting a pastor. It was the UCC's turn to have someone from its ranks, and Dirk happily accepted the call. Dirk stayed at the churches for six years, but conflict over one thing or another was the norm.

At his first service in the UCC church, twelve people attended. The average age of members was seventy-five. They seemed to want a chaplain rather than a minister to lead them into growth; but Dirk wanted the church to grow. The previous minister had been a practicing homosexual, which Dirk found abhorrent and unbiblical, but the church people did not seem to be bothered by it.

51

The American Baptist Church was the stronger of the two with about thirty active members. This church was theologically diverse with members who were fundamentalist in their beliefs alongside members who were outspokenly liberal. One of the fundamentalist couples reacted strongly against Dirk's preaching and teaching of Reformed doctrine since they felt Wesleyan teaching was more biblical. This couple worked hard to undermine Dirk's credibility behind his back. He felt the lack of trust from people and did not know why.

On the other hand, the more liberal people saw nothing wrong with having an organist who was not a Christian and who was living with a man outside of marriage. When Dirk and the elders talked with her about this, she left the church in anger. That upset others in the church who said the private life of the organist was no one's business.

On another occasion a single man in the church impregnated a single woman in the church and they decided to live together without getting married. Dirk went to talk with the couple, and they loudly and angrily said, "Who are you to tell us what to do? This is none of your business!" Some people in the church felt these situations should have been dealt with by Dirk and the leaders, but others suggested that Dirk ignore them.

In spite of the UCC growing from twelve to thirty people attending worship on Sundays, the leaders eventually asked Dirk to leave. They did not like his conservative approach to ministry and biblical teaching. They also broke the yoke with the ABC and decided to obtain a part-time UCC minister on their own.

When this happened, the leaders of the Baptist church met to discuss their new situation. The leaders asked Dirk not to attend these meetings, saying, "We don't want to burden you with a discussion about finances, and besides, we need to develop some leadership of our own." Dirk learned later that the discussions focused on how to get him to leave.

He was disheartened that the leaders did not deal honestly with him. Finances were a serious problem in the church, even though attendance at Sunday worship had gone from thirty to ninety under Dirk's leadership. Had it not been for Julie's working as a nurse, Dirk and Julie would not have made it financially.

With finances tight and the relationship with the Baptist church strained, Dirk decided it was time to seek a call elsewhere. The conflict had taken a toll on him, and he had begun to wonder if he had the gifts for ministry. Julie was even more hurt by the conflict. She did not have a strong background in the church to start with and could not believe that people who considered themselves Christians would act the way they did. As they prayed and talked about their situation, Julie and Dirk wondered if it might be better if he worked as an assistant pastor under a seasoned minister, and in a church more closely aligned to their theological beliefs. So it was with anticipation that Dirk eventually considered a call to Faith Congregational Church of Des Moines, Iowa.

Dirk's name had been given to the Des Moines church by a denominational official who was aware of Dirk's difficulties at the yoked parish and who saw a good match between Dirk and Faith Church in their theology and practice. Des Moines was not in a part of the country Dirk was particularly attracted to, and he was more interested in renewal ministry than working in an established evangelical church, but he felt it best to work in a church where there did not appear to be conflict and he could work under a seasoned minister. It would also be good for Julie, providing relief from the stress they were under.

During the candidating process Dirk immediately liked Gordon, the senior minister. Gordon was confident, experienced, an excellent preacher, and good in pastoral care. As a naturally outgoing person, Gordon drew people to him, and Dirk sensed he would enjoy being on staff with him.

The job description for the associate pastor called for 50 percent of the time to be spent with youth and young adults and 50 percent on general pastoral work. When the church voted to call Dirk, he quickly responded in the affirmative. And Dirk, Julie, and their two preschool children said their tearful good-byes to friends in their first parish and moved to Des Moines.

Faith Congregational Church had a long, stable history. It had been affiliated with the more conservative branch of the Evangelical and Reformed denomination that merged with the Congregationalists years ago to form the UCC. Only two pastors had served the church over the last sixty-six years, and Gordon was in his eighth year as the senior minister when Dirk arrived. Although the church listed one thousand members on the roll, average attendance on Sundays for worship was four hundred. Many of the church families were well established in the community, and many had been members of the church for years. All in all, Dirk saw it as a place to heal his wounds, gain more experience, and enjoy a different kind of ministry.

Dirk's ministry at Faith Church began on a good note. He and Gordon hit it off well. They met regularly for devotions and to discuss theology and denominational issues. Gordon was active in the renewal movement in the UCC, and since Dirk was also interested in these matters, they had much to talk about. Gordon told Dirk he was thinking of retiring in two years at the age of sixty and devoting himself full-time to the travel business with his wife, Virginia. He hinted that Dirk would be the logical one to become the senior minister. (UCC polity would allow this to happen.) Dirk did not think too much about it, but he was flattered that Gordon considered him capable of being the senior minister.

In his second month at the church, Dirk reviewed with Gordon his plans for an upcoming retreat for young adults. Dirk had concentrated on a theme of spiritual nurture for the retreat, but Gordon and his two grown children, a son age twenty-six and a daughter age twenty-four, who were active in the group, thought a social emphasis would be better. They reasoned that the church ministry in general gave numerous opportunities for spiritual nurture, but there were few social events for the young adults. In the end they compromised, combining both social fun and discussion on spiritual matters. Dirk saw this planning meeting as a friendly discussion characterized by an easy give-and-take, and nothing like what he had been through in the past. Afterward, he sensed that it put some kind of wedge between him and Gordon. Gordon began to withdraw from him. Dirk was confused by this and hoped it was not the beginning of a rift between him and Gordon. He wanted no part of conflict ever again.

Several months later, Dirk heard rumors circulating within the congregation about fraudulent actions by Gordon and Virginia in their travel business. When he heard this, Dirk recalled that a few days after he arrived at the church, the chair of the search committee said to him that he hoped it was not a mistake to bring Dirk on staff at that time since they were having some problems with the senior minister. Dirk thought little of it at the time, but now he wondered if this is what the committee chair had been referring to.

The travel agency where Gordon and Virginia worked had accused them of not turning in all the money they had collected from people who had taken trips led by Gordon and Virginia. Instead of telling people to write checks payable to the travel agency, as was company policy, Virginia had checks made payable to her. She, in turn, paid the travel agency. When the agency owners accused her of withholding some of the money, Virginia countercharged that she had not been fully paid by the agency. The trips in question, all pleasure trips, primarily involved people from Faith Church. Gordon and Virginia enjoyed leading the trips and seeing different parts of the world—with all expenses covered.

The charge against Gordon and Virginia had been brought by a woman from the church who also worked for the travel agency, a job she got through Virginia's influence. The agency stated it wanted the matter resolved quickly so as not to hurt its business or discredit the good reputation Gordon and Faith Church had in the community. The agency claimed Gordon and Virginia owed between ten and twelve thousand dollars. When the owner first approached Gordon and Virginia in private about the problem, they indicated a willingness to straighten out the situation quickly, but after some time went by and nothing happened, the woman went to the church elders.

The elders immediately set up a meeting with Gordon and Virginia. As an elder, Dirk attended the meeting and observed that Virginia appeared ready to talk openly about the details, but Gordon cautioned her to say nothing. Gordon said they had done nothing wrong, although they may have committed a "business error," as he called it. The meeting ended without any decision or action being taken.

The next day Dirk asked Gordon if they could talk about the matter. Gordon said it was the agency's fault, not his or Virginia's. Dirk had a strong sense that Gordon was not interested in talking about it, so he dropped the matter. Dirk did not reveal that after the meeting ended the night before, one elder said to the others lingering in the room that he thought Gordon had "sinned" in the matter, but he did not know what they could do about it. Dirk had hoped to be able to talk frankly with Gordon about the whole situation, including the elder's remark. Dirk felt frustrated that the issue was not resolved and knew from his first church that unresolved conflict could rear its ugly head in destructive ways later.

Within a few days rumors were flying all over the church about the situation. Dirk wondered where people got their information and why it could not be talked about openly since everyone seemed to know about it. But he had observed already the unspoken rule in the church that problems of any sort would not be dealt with openly. Still, he had also observed a strong sense of trust in and commitment to the pastoral leadership. "Touch not the Lord's anointed" was the clear attitude of the church.

Some of the elders and a few other people in the church came to Dirk to ask for advice about what to do. Dirk felt torn between a sense of loyalty to Gordon and his desire for no further harm to come to the church. Even though Dirk was not the focus of the conflict, he felt like he was being drawn into it. He didn't know what to say when church people, who may or may not have known about the details, would say things like "The pastor doesn't seem to be well; is he okay?" Dirk himself had noticed that Gordon's preaching was lackluster and that he appeared tired and drawn. And certainly he was not the dynamic person he had been before the controversy started. Several people remarked that the quality of Gordon's pastoral care was not what it used to be.

A month or two after the first elders meeting in which the charge of business fraud had been presented, Dirk went to Gordon and pleaded with him to talk about the matter with someone. Gordon remained silent. Dirk decided the only course of action for the good of the church was to ask the elders to meet again to discuss the situation. He was convinced that well-meaning Christians could come together, love each other, accept one another's failures, pray, and find a satisfactory solution to the problem.

So a second meeting of the elders was called, and Gordon was present without Virginia. Dirk had wanted to assert leadership in resolving the difficulty when it appeared to him no progress was being made. He had talked to several people to get information about the problem and he also knew that two elders had gone to the travel agency to get the agency's complete side of the story. Dirk presented his information,

57

which included a rather widespread perception that Gordon and Virginia were in the wrong on the matter. He also invited the two elders to present their findings, but they declined. This surprised Dirk since he knew their information would corroborate his findings. Dirk had hoped at the meeting that Gordon would repent and seek restitution, but to his dismay Gordon became angry, accused the elders of making him a victim, and angrily accused Dirk of turning against him. He abruptly walked out of the meeting. Dirk was stunned.

After Gordon walked out, the elders decided to write him and Virginia a letter, stating on the one hand their love for and commitment to them as pastor and wife, but on the other hand their desire to see the matter resolved with the agency. They requested that Gordon and Virginia go to the travel agency and resolve the matter directly. The letter also stated that it appeared to the elders that some repayment of money to the agency was necessary.

After Gordon left, one of the elders stated he thought Gordon had "morally erred," but no one wanted to say that directly to Gordon or put it in the letter. The situation was made all the more awkward by Gordon's son being one of the elders, and he was either silent in the discussion or staunchly defended his father.

In the days following this meeting, Gordon avoided speaking to Dirk, except at one point when he blamed Dirk for stirring up the leaders against him. Gordon said Satan was using it to bring down his ministry. By now Dirk was wondering himself if he had done harm to Gordon and the ministry. He wondered if he should have taken a passive role in the conflict and been more supportive of the pastor. The latter would have been difficult for Dirk, however, since his investigation of the situation led him to believe Gordon had some guilt in the matter.

Dirk was in his eighth month at the church and was wondering if he would survive much longer. A few leaders had made remarks to the effect that they would not blame him if he decided to leave. Dirk was never sure whether they were suggesting that he leave or sympathizing with his dilemma. He found it difficult to talk frankly with those who made such comments. Their attitude was "You're the leader; you decide what to do." But he knew that when he had asserted leadership by calling the elders together, it had gone badly, and he was being blamed for that.

Others said that they hoped Dirk would not leave, that they needed him to help see them through this difficulty, and they appeared to depend on him to decide what to do. Dirk felt trapped and it was affecting his freedom to minister in the church. It was also affecting Julie, and consequently, his marriage. Julie now wondered if there was any situation where "Christians behaved like Christians," as she put it. She was also homesick for friends and family in the Pacific Northwest. Dirk had to admit that he was homesick too.

Dirk mentioned to Gordon he was thinking of leaving the church. Gordon appeared relieved as he quietly said to Dirk, "I will help you in any way I can." They never talked about it again, however.

As Dirk and Julie talked and prayed, four options emerged:

1. Stay with the church, help the people work through the conflict, and then leave.
2. Stay with the church. Hope that Gordon would leave soon and that Dirk might be considered for the position of senior pastor.
3. Take a group from the church and begin a new work. A few people had suggested as much, but he had reservations about participating in a church split.
4. Begin immediately to seek another place of ministry and leave Faith Church as soon as possible.

As he reviewed his options, the old feelings of inadequacy and failure stirred within his soul. In a few hours he would be at the elders meeting, the third one called to address the situation with Gordon. It had now been two months since the elders had sent their letter to Gordon, and nothing had been done by Gordon and Virginia. The elders had reluctantly decided to try once again to address the matter. Dirk was dreading the meeting. *What should I do?* he asked himself.

4

You're a Snot-Nosed Young Pastor!

Authority/Leadership Conflict

*E*d returned to his office dejected. He had just finished the regular monthly meeting of the board of deacons of Faith Baptist Church, where he was the senior pastor. The church was affiliated with the American Baptist Churches in the USA and was located in a large town in south-central Pennsylvania. The board of deacons, composed of both men and women, had oversight over all affairs of the church. Ed had thought he had the support of the board, but now he wasn't sure.

Two weeks earlier Ed had requested that the deacons meet in a special session to discuss the disruptive and manipulative behavior of Margaret, one of the longtime Sunday school teachers in the church. But on the day the meeting was to be held, Harry, one of the twenty-four deacons in the church, stopped by Ed's office and tried to convince Ed he was in a battle he would lose. This surprised Ed. He thought most of the deacons were relieved that the issue of Margaret's behavior would finally be discussed. When Harry said, "You better find out who's on your team!" implying that Ed might not have the support of the deacons, Ed decided to cancel the special meeting and let the deacons themselves bring up the matter at the regular monthly meeting. At that meeting, just concluded, no one had said anything about Margaret.

Ed sat in the semidarkness of his office and wondered if he should leave the church. He recalled the Sunday he candidated to be the pastor, how he had been overwhelmed with emotion, so much so that he cried when the church voted him in. He had a strong sense within his spirit that God had led him to be the senior pastor of Faith Baptist Church, and that had sustained him on several occasions already in his brief year and a half at the church. But now he was beginning to wonder if he had missed God's call, if God was saying it was time to leave, if he should stick it out and try to effect change, or if he should just ignore it all and attend to other pastoral tasks. It seemed to him there had been nothing but conflict since he had arrived, and it was taking its toll on him.

The church had a crisis of authority. In the conversation Ed had with Harry two days earlier, Harry said, "You are creating division in the church, and this means you are listening to Satan!" Ed reached for his Bible and read aloud from Matthew 18 and 1 Corinthians 5. He told Harry he was attempting to follow scriptural guidelines in handling the problem with Margaret. Harry interrupted him, "I find that culturally offensive. Those passages do not apply today." This stunned Ed. The church was conservative in theology and held to a high view of Scripture as the authoritative guide for godly living today.

When Harry left Ed's office, he said curtly, "Call off the meeting, and do it now. It will take longer to get rid of Margaret than to get you out. You can be out of here in sixty days!"

Ed sighed and wondered what he would tell his wife, Lisa, when he got home. She was aware of the ongoing conflict and was concerned about how it was affecting Ed. She had observed that he had been a bit morose lately, in contrast with his normally optimistic and upbeat demeanor.

Lately she had noticed a distance between herself and Ed. They talked about it and reaffirmed their love for each other. Neither of them wanted the stress of the church conflict to affect their relationship with each other or to color how their two children, ages five and three, viewed the church. Ed and Lisa observed that it had been quite a while since they had laughed together, and they vowed to find enjoyment with each other despite the problems at church.

The problem with Margaret began almost the day that Ed began as pastor of the church. At his ordination several years ago, one of the speakers had said, "Beware the first person who invites you to dinner. That person may have an agenda." Margaret had been the first to invite Ed and his family to dinner. But as Ed saw it, the problem was not just with Margaret. The problem was with how the church viewed discipline and biblical guidelines for living.

For example, prior to Ed's coming to the church, the custodian had accused the youth minister of having an affair with one of the volunteer nursery workers. When the leaders investigated the charge, they found it was false, and they removed the custodian from his position. Prior to this job, the man had spent time in prison for drunkenness and robbery, and although the church wanted to give him a chance to make good, this incident demonstrated to some people his continuing instability.

But Margaret stirred up people in the church by raising the issue in her adult Sunday school class. "What kind of a church would do this to a person?" she asked. The class averaged ten to fifteen people each week and was supposed to discuss contemporary issues. Class members became so alarmed over the firing of the custodian that they pressured the deacons to rehire the man, which they did.

Margaret, age sixty, had taught Sunday school for most of her forty years in the church. Some people had warned Ed when he came that she was a powerful influence in the church and was often dogmatic and opinionated. Ed sensed that people wanted to see something done about it but didn't know what to do.

So Ed decided early on that he would sit in on Margaret's class. On one occasion a bright young man who regularly attended the class spoke up and mildly disagreed with Margaret. The young man was shy, but Ed thought his point was excellent and was communicated in a humble and winsome way. But Margaret responded testily, "Who died and made you God!" The young man was crestfallen and soon left the church. When Ed suggested to the Christian education board that something should be done about Margaret's behavior, the board chairperson agreed but said she did not want to bring up the matter herself.

Another example of the problem the church had with authority was an episode with a former deacon. The man resigned from the board when he was going through a divorce. He moved in with the woman with whom he was having an affair. The two of them came to church regularly and sat in the front row, proud as peacocks, it seemed to Ed. Ed went to talk to the couple. He tried to talk about repentance, forgiveness, and the need to live godly lives, but they would have none of it. They indicated to Ed they had no intention of changing their behavior—or leaving the church. Somehow Margaret heard about the incident and made it the focus of her class the following Sunday. "How many of you want to be part of a church where they throw people out?" she asked.

As before, class members pressured the deacons to leave the couple alone. At a deacons meeting when Ed broached the subject of what Margaret had done, one of the deacons said, "Margaret is an abrasive person, but she is also much loved. She has taught many of us through the years. We know she speaks her mind and doesn't care who she offends, but if we leave her alone, she'll wind down. Besides, she's nice to more people than she offends." True, Margaret did reach out to people. When someone new visited the church or there was an illness or death in a family within the church, Margaret was there, bringing food and offering to help.

In another incident several parents told Ed they were no longer allowing their fifth and sixth grade children to go to Sunday school because the teacher of their class, a woman who had taught the class for close to forty years, was no longer effective. She was slipping mentally.

The chairperson of the Christian education board came to Ed and asked if he could do anything about the problem. So with the support of the Christian education board, Ed went to talk with the woman and told her how some of the children and parents were feeling. He suggested several places in the church where her gifts could be used and where help was needed—such as baking bread and taking it to new-comers or helping with the church's food pantry—but she would have none of it.

She told Margaret about the conversation with Ed. Once again Margaret made this the focus of her class the follow-ing Sunday. She said, "The leadership of this church wants to throw out old people. Is this the kind of church you want to belong to?" Class members then lobbied the deacons to get Ed to "mind his own business and leave people alone."

Ed weighed his options. He could ignore Margaret, as others in the church did and encouraged him to do, but he feared this would only make matters worse. He had observed that people were cautious about engaging in new ministry ventures out of fear for how Margaret would react. Ed was convinced that if the church was going to move forward, they could not ignore her misconduct. After spending much time in prayer he made an appointment to see Margaret in her home.

He began the conversation by affirming her concern for and hospitality towards people. He thanked her for her many years of teaching. Then he turned the conversation to the problems he saw. Her demeanor changed dramatically. Before he could get very far, she attacked him verbally in a way he had never seen anyone do before. She was out of control, so hostile and irrational that he wondered if it was demonic (a thought he was not given to easily although he believed it could happen). Her words and tone were so vicious that it actually frightened him. He prayed for strength and courage, and asked if she would please listen to what he had to say.

Margaret calmed down and said she would listen. Once again he pointed out several of her gifts and contributions to the church through the years, but he also cited several instances where she had hurt people. He asked if she would consider changing the focus of her class to a Bible study, but before he could finish his sentence, she interrupted with a rapid-fire litany of accusations against him, none of which was true.

"You're a snot-nosed young pastor who wants to control the church!" she said. "You hate gray! You're a horrible pastor! You preach terrible sermons, and you've done nothing but create a climate of despair in the church since you came!"

Her words stung. On the one hand Ed knew she was being irrational, but she was hitting where he felt weakest.

When Ed came to Faith Baptist a year and a half ago, he was surprised that a church this size—eight hundred members with an average attendance on Sundays around three hundred—would call him to be the senior pastor. He was only twenty-nine at the time and had served previously as an assistant pastor for four years at another Baptist church following his graduation from seminary. In that church Ed had worked primarily with Christian education and youth, enjoying considerable success in both ministries. When a new pastor came to that church who did not work well with Ed, Ed took that as a sign from God that he should move on. He was growing in his desire to do the broad work of the pastor. So he began to seek other possibilities in his denomination.

That's when Faith Baptist Church contacted him. Faith Baptist had a full-time youth minister, a full-time secretary, a full-time custodian, and a part-time music director. The size of the church and the varied ministries and programs were impressive. Ed thought it would be a good experience to proceed with the candidating process, but he never dreamed he would end up being the primary candidate.

Ed, who had an M.Div., learned early on in the candidating process that he was the only person without an earned doctorate being considered by the committee. He wondered why they pointed that out. Did they think they could control him better since he was relatively young and inexperienced for a church of this size?

As Margaret talked, Ed's mind flashed back to the phone call he made to the pastor who preceded him at the church. This man came to Faith Baptist also at the age of twenty-nine and stayed twelve years. Ed telephoned him after receiving the call from the congregation to be the pastor (a 92 percent favorable vote out of 250 voting), but before he accepted the offer he wanted to know how the ministry had gone with his predecessor and if there was anything he should be aware of. His predecessor said with feeling, "They're good people, but if you cross them, they'll never forgive you."

The previous pastor added that although his ministry at Faith Baptist went well, it did so because he learned that to get anything done he had to do it himself. "Working through the power structure doesn't accomplish anything," he said.

The search committee told Ed that there had been some dissatisfaction with the former pastor because he tended to make unilateral decisions. He once signed a contract with a construction company for three hundred thousand dollars without congregational approval. Only the board of trustees could approve spending this amount of money, and only after the congregation had voted to do it by a two-thirds majority. But the pastor said that it was the only way he could get things moving, so he signed the contract himself and the work was done. The congregation eventually went along with it, but there was a great deal of unhappiness with the pastor. It was clear to Ed that they did not want him to repeat the actions of his predecessor.

All of this went through his mind when Margaret called him a "snot-nosed young pastor." He asked himself, *Am I really trying to control the church as she says?* What he wanted was for Margaret's class to study the Bible and not be a forum to criticize him and the leadership of the church. He wanted Christ's love and presence to permeate the church, something that did not seem to be happening, and he thought Margaret's control of others was a partial reason. Even though the class numbered only ten, they wielded extensive influence.

After Margaret finished her accusations, Ed gently asked if she would be accountable to him as pastor and also to the Christian education board. Again Margaret exploded. "I will be accountable to no one but Jesus, and I will not listen to *you* anymore!" Ed said he was sorry they could not agree but hoped they could talk further soon.

As he got up to leave, she reached out and gave him a hard hug. That surprised him so much he did not know how to respond. As he was driving home, he thought, *When she hugged me, it felt like a dagger in my back.* He was exhausted in a way he had never felt before.

At home he told Lisa about the incident, and they prayed for direction. A few days later Ed told the deacons what had happened and discovered they already knew about it. Comments such as "That's the way Margaret is" and "Don't rock the boat" punctuated their conversation. They said

Margaret was telling everyone in the church about the incident and was expressing doubts over whether Ed ought to be their pastor. Rumors had started floating through the church that Ed would be leaving soon. Ed received anonymously a copy of a *Time* magazine article entitled "Busybodies and Crybabies." An attached note asked, "Do you know anyone like this?"

Although the deacons thought Ed should ignore the situation, they supported Ed's asking an executive consultant who was a member of the church to go with Ed to talk with Margaret. This man, however, refused the request, saying that something needed to be done, but either the Christian education board or the deacons should handle it. So the deacons agreed for one of them to accompany Ed to talk with Margaret and to request that she stop using the Sunday school class as a forum to criticize the leadership. When Ed telephoned her to set up a time to meet, she angrily stated she had no intention of changing her class or of seeing Ed or anyone else. She hung up the phone before Ed could say anything else.

Now what do I do? Ed asked himself. He wondered if this was the battle he should be willing to go to the wall for. His unsuccessful attempts at curtailing Margaret's power had only given her more power. He wanted to be faithful to God, but he wasn't sure what that meant in this circumstance. Margaret was a person Christ died for just as Christ had died for him. Both he and she were sinners in need of grace. But what about the welfare of the church and its ministry in the world?

The church was at a crucial point in its obedience to the Lord. As the pastor, he needed to lead the church even though he felt emotionally, physically, and spiritually drained. *Where is God in all this?* he asked himself. *What does God want me to do?*

5

Norm Was Fired

Depression/Anger

*I*t had now been five years since Norm had been fired by Trinity Baptist Church of Springfield, Rhode Island. He knew he should say he resigned because that's what he did, but the resignation had been requested by the church leaders. Even though the firing had taken place five years ago, Norm was still shocked by the whole matter. Discussing his firing with a seminary professor, he said, "I didn't know they could do that. I thought only moral failure could cause termination, and that was certainly not the case with me!"

Adding to the shock was the fact that he still had not been able to find another church to serve as pastor. He enjoyed the occasional supply preaching that came his way, but he wanted to be a pastor again. Now fifty-four years old, he wondered if that would ever happen again.

Being in his fifties, not pastoring for the last five years, and being fired from his previous church—even if he did say resigned—did not exactly make him marketable to churches. It all seemed so unfair and certainly was not what he expected when he graduated from seminary and took his first church twenty-eight years ago. The last few years had been his "dark night of the soul," a time frequently visited by anger and depression. How had it come to this?

At age seventeen Norm had become a Christian in the Baptist church that his mother, stepbrother, and he attended in Nashua, New Hampshire. Shortly after that, in his freshman year of college, he sensed God calling him into full-time Christian service. He remembered how strong an inner conviction it had been—and still was. After graduating from a private secular college in Maine with a B.A. in philosophy and religion, he went on to seminary in Massachusetts, where he received his M.Div. degree three years later. He spent the summer after graduation doing clinical pastoral education at a hospital in the Boston area.

In September, Norm accepted a call to be the pastor of a church affiliated with the Baptist Union of Western Canada. It was a new church being started by the home missions program of the denomination and was being sponsored by a larger church in the area, which sent twenty-five people as a core group for the new church. Around forty people soon attended the new church, and Norm and his wife, Connie, were happy there.

Then disaster struck. Fire gutted their building. The fire put a strain on finances for the small church and hurt the morale of the people. Norm began to experience tension with leaders and others in the church. It seemed like a struggle for who would control the church. One woman in particular, the Sunday school superintendent, was very assertive and raised questions about Norm's style of leadership. There was widespread discontent with his occasional practice of giving an invitation to accept Christ at the end of the morning service. Disagreements over theology added to the tension.

Some people dropped hints that it might be time for Norm to find another church, which both surprised and hurt him since he had planned to stay at the church a long time. He had enjoyed his relationship with the pastor of the sponsoring church; the man had been a mentor to him. After being there only four and a half years, however, Norm decided he should move on. He accepted a call to be the pastor of a Baptist church in a large city in central Canada. He left his first church with feelings of sadness and regret. It had not worked out the way he expected. He had not been well taught in the area of church politics, but he was not sure playing politics in church was what he wanted to do, anyway. Conflict made him uncomfortable, so he was glad for the opportunity to go to another church.

In the process of moving to the new church, Norm, Connie, and their three children were caught in a massive blizzard that marooned them for three days in a small motel room. The idea of moving hadn't been well received by his children, and this only intensified the trauma of the move. Their oldest daughter was a senior in high school and was not happy at having to transfer to another school in April of her final year. Nor did it help that Norm finished one Sunday in the first church and began the next Sunday in the new church.

Life and ministry soon went well overall, however. The congregation numbered almost two hundred with a broad age spread. The church had many active programs as well as a good evangelistic ministry. Norm called it his "Philippian church" experience. He felt supported in every way. The people followed his leadership with enthusiasm. The camp program and music ministry of the church were especially strong.

In spite of his immense pleasure in pastoring this church, after seven years Norm felt it was time to move on. He accepted a call to pastor an American Baptist church in the northeast part of the United States.

Moving back to the States again took some adjusting for Norm and Connie and their children. The open culture and freer lifestyle of Americans contrasted with the conservative stance of Canadians. Theological pluralism in the ABC and the diversity reflected in this particular local church were also difficult for Norm to handle. His soul was in constant ferment towards American culture and the church—and occasionally even his family. Now and then this ferment spilled into the open.

The most serious conflict in this church centered on the desire of a small group of people for a more charismatic expression of worship and teaching. Hard lines were drawn between those who wanted this emphasis and those who did not. Norm tried hard to work out compromises between the two groups. He was willing to allow the charismatic group to organize parallel programs with a charismatic flavor alongside the regular programs of the church. Nevertheless in the end around a dozen people left the church to form a charismatic fellowship.

Although there was some measure of relief in the church when those people left, Norm was criticized by people in both groups for his leadership in the conflict. For his part, Norm had felt caught in the middle. Nothing he proposed worked out. Some people criticized him for being stubborn and rigid and said he was too tenacious in defending his ideas. Others said he did not act decisively enough.

In his sixth year at the church, the criticism increased. A growing number of people from the Christian college in the community raised questions about Norm's ability to lead the church. Criticism also focused on the worship service and his preaching. He was seen as a traditional pastor, and many people wanted a more contemporary worship service. Norm admitted he did like a more traditional style of worship and preaching, and he felt that was what he did best. One leader said to him, "Things went well under your leadership for a while, but you should have left two years ago!" As tensions grew, people started leaving the church and the financial giving level dropped drastically. The congregation that numbered 350 when Norm came dwindled to a much smaller group that had difficulty providing financial support for Norm and the church's ministry. When the leaders expressed concern over the number of people leaving, Norm said, "It's their decision. If they want to leave the church, let them."

Unbeknownst to the church, Norm had been looking for a new pastorate for some time. His area minister had also encouraged him to leave, so it was with a sense of relief that Norm accepted a call to Trinity Baptist Church in Springfield, Rhode Island. He hoped his fourth church would be better.

At Trinity Baptist Church, the first year and a half went well for Norm. Then conflict surfaced when the church hired a new staff person to work with the Christian education program. Trinity Baptist was the first church the new assistant had served in, and Norm saw the "church bosses," as he called them, drawing the new assistant into their circle, manipulating him to do what they wanted when they could not get Norm to do what they wanted. In fact, Norm felt the "bosses" began to move the assistant into the foreground of decision making and leadership and to push Norm to the fringes of influence in the church. The assistant pastor appeared unaware of what was happening.

Then major conflict arose that had nothing to do with the assistant pastor. The daughter of a prominent family in the church, whose mother was chair of the trustee board, asked Norm to officiate at her wedding. Norm's practice was to have six premarital counseling sessions with engaged couples before the wedding, but the young woman refused to do this. Then Norm discovered she was living with her fiancé and was unwilling to move out.

When Norm brought up the matter at the deacons meeting, one of the deacons said, "The wedding *will* be held in this church! The only decision you have to make is whether or not you will officiate." Norm went to the young woman's mother to explain his position. She called him a prude and noted, "It's normal for young people to live together today." Norm went back to the diaconate and suggested as a compromise that a retired minister in the area who had been the interim pastor at Trinity before Norm came be asked to perform the ceremony; meanwhile Norm would go on vacation the week of the wedding. This is what happened, but that incident forever changed his relationship with the leader.

A few months after the wedding incident, Norm was informed at a regular deacons meeting that he was out of a job. When he asked why, the deacons gave five reasons:

1. He spent too much time studying.
2. His sermons were too long.
3. His sermons were too complicated for people to follow.
4. He did not visit people enough.
5. He was not active enough in denominational activities.

During the meeting he repeatedly asked for forgiveness for where he had fallen short of their expectations, but they did not extend it to him. He also said he would think about what they were saying and would make every effort to improve, but several of the deacons said it was too late for that. When the vote was taken at the end of the meeting, it was a call for his resignation. A few deacons had expressed support for Norm during the meeting, but they were won over by the strong voices of the others. The vote requesting his resignation was unanimous.

The timing of the firing was upsetting to Norm. Connie was away from home leading a women's retreat, and Norm did not want to call her with news that would certainly ruin the retreat for her. So he called his area minister, who met with him and explored his options. Three options surfaced:

1. Norm could resign effective immediately and ask to negotiate for salary and parsonage living arrangements for a few more months while he looked for another church.
2. He could give a two-month notice, as the constitution of the church called for when a pastor resigned. While this would guarantee salary and parsonage accommodations for at least two months, that might not be long enough to find another church.
3. He could put the matter to the congregation for discussion. The congregation could then vote to declare its will in the matter. The process for doing this was outlined in the constitution. This would mean Norm would not resign but would allow the congregation to determine what he should do.

The deacons meeting had been held on a Tuesday, and Connie would return home the following Saturday. Those four days were agonizing for Norm. He spent a great deal of time jogging in an effort to deal with inner feelings so intense that he was unable to label them. He spent much time thinking through the options he and the area minister had discussed. By the time Connie returned home, he had decided on a combination of options two and three.

Norm discovered that not all the deacons had been informed about the meeting in which his resignation was requested and so were not present. Norm felt he had been set up by certain deacons, and he knew the congregation had to vote on the termination of a pastor. The deacons only had the right to question his leadership and advise him to resign.

Thinking that the congregation would support him and vote to refuse his resignation if he offered it, Norm did resign. Two weeks later the congregation met to act on the resignation. Norm expected a discussion on the issues, but to his surprise the congregation not only did not discuss his resignation, they accepted it without a dissenting vote. The constitutional process would be followed, making his resignation effective in two months.

To make matters worse, on the Sunday Norm read his resignation letter to the congregation, their son, age nineteen, was seriously hurt in a car accident. (Fortunately the son eventually made a complete recovery from his injuries.) Norm and Connie were reeling. What was going on? Where was God in all this? Why would people do this to them? Where would they go? How would this affect the children?

The area minister spent much time with Norm in the days following the congregational meeting, providing necessary structure at a time when everything was collapsing around him. But tragedy struck again when the area minister died of a heart attack. Norm felt numb.

Before the area minister died, he made arrangements for Norm to work at the regional camp operated by the American Baptist churches. This was an immediate help to Norm since he had only six weeks before his housing and salary were terminated. Although his file was being circulated to ABC churches, he had received no calls. At the camp they had a modest place to live and received a monetary stipend. Connie found a job as a teacher's aide, and the profit they had invested from the sale of their previous house supplemented their income, making it possible to meet expenses. The camp job also enabled them to stay in the area for another year while their youngest son finished high school.

A feeling of numbness lingered in Norm's heart. It did not help that during the year Norm worked at the camp, he and Connie drove by the empty parsonage of Trinity Baptist Church several times a week as they drove Connie to work. It was a constant and painful reminder of what had happened.

After Norm served a year as camp director, his job was phased out in a money-saving move by the denomination. No church had opened up yet, although he had been diligently looking. Norm and Connie did occasional house-sitting for people on vacation, and Norm engaged in supply preaching as often as possible. After leaving the camp, they found a small house to rent. After two months, however, the owner decided to sell the house. They found a small beach house to rent and made another move.

In his search for direction after being fired from Trinity Baptist Church, Norm talked with few people about his situation. He spent considerable time instead in Bible reading, meditation, and prayer. At one point, though, he talked with two former professors from his seminary days. They encouraged him to consider enrolling in further graduate study as a means of engaging his mind and sorting out where God might be leading him in the future. Following a time of reflection and prayer, Norm decided to enter the D.Min. program of his alma mater.

Early in his D.Min. studies, as a result of the reading and written work required in one course, he identified a persistent feeling that he had not been able to label previously but that he had been carrying around in his inner being for years. It had a name, he now realized, and that name was anger. Up to this point he had been unwilling to admit being angry about anything, but looking back over the years of his pastoral ministry he knew that it was anger that he had felt on numerous occasions. He didn't know what to do with it. He didn't think good Christians got angry, especially pastors, so he had engaged in denial. Admitting anger was hard, expressing it was unthinkable, so Norm had kept it to himself.

He was beginning to realize, however, that he had paid a high price for internalizing anger. For years he had suffered with gastrointestinal problems—gas pain, indigestion, and a peptic ulcer. His blood pressure was high. Thinking about it now, he recalled several occasions when Connie had inquired whether he was angry about something, and he had always denied it. Or she would observe that he appeared

79

angry, and she would try to get him to talk about it with her, but again he would deny it. He realized he had rejected his wife's sensitive care.

After recognizing that he was angry, it did not take long for Norm to figure out that the church and particular people in the church were the focus of his anger. He reasoned that he had a right to be angry at the church for what he had been through during his pastoral ministry. And even though he was looking for a place to serve as a pastor, there were times when he was not sure he really wanted to do it. He was afraid the same thing that had happened before would happen again. He wasn't sure he could trust people. He was wary of people who tried to control others, and it seemed to him that this tendency was true of most church leaders.

While Norm was not engaged in formal ministry, he found he had a ministry to other people who were turned off by the church. He was having more contact with non-Christians and former churchgoers who were angry at the church than he had ever had when he was a pastor. He wondered if this was the ministry God really wanted him involved in.

Norm knew that Connie and the children were also angry at the church. One of their sons had become engaged to a Roman Catholic woman and had said to Norm and Connie, "Why should I stay with the Baptist church after what they did to Dad?" Since leaving Trinity Baptist Church, Norm and Connie had been attending another Baptist church, but neither of them could bring themselves to call the minister of the church "pastor." To them, Norm was still the pastor of the family. And they had never been able to request that their names be removed from the membership rolls at Trinity.

In his readings for one of his counseling courses, Norm came across material that described the passive-aggressive person. The article noted that this was a character trait of many ministers. Norm admitted that some of the characteristics were true of him: resistance to perceived demands from others, social and occupational ineffectiveness (sometimes called "intentional inefficiency"), stubbornness, and persisting in the behavior in circumstances where more self-assertive and effective behavior are possible. He definitely did not like for others to make demands on him. He even resisted academic deadlines, often submitting his work late. As he thought further about it, he realized that on many occasions throughout his ministry people had accused him of not being willing to conform to the expectations of others even when it was not a matter of principle; he would follow his own agenda. Norm would be hurt by this criticism but would wear it as a badge of honor—he was called to follow God not meet people's expectations. In conflict situations he had always seen himself as being in the right.

In a conversation Norm had with a professor about his anger and passive-aggressive tendencies, the professor asked Norm if he thought he was depressed. The professor pointed out that depression is often linked to anger and passive-aggressive behavior, and Norm showed signs of being depressed. Norm admitted he was discouraged by not receiving a call from any church in the last five years, that anger was a strong emotion within him, and that he was most likely a passive-aggressive person; but he was fairly sure depression was not a part of his being. For one thing, he felt good Christians did not get depressed. For another, he saw depression as an incapacitating thing, and he did not think this was the case with him, although he was often down. More than anything else he felt lonely. Were it not for Connie and the good times they had together, he did not know how he would have survived the last five years— or how he would make it in the future. Spending much time in Bible reading, prayer, and reflection also provided a strong base of support for him. Besides God and Connie, however, there was no one he trusted or wanted to talk to.

And so Norm waited, not entirely sure what he was waiting for. He was enjoying a quiet life with Connie and was pleased to see how much she enjoyed her job and how much more confident she had become. Connie said Norm was a more enjoyable person to be with now that he wasn't a pastor. He was more relaxed and less preoccupied. Connie's salary and the income from the housing investment provided for a modest living.

So from one point of view, life was good. But Norm admitted that at times he longed to be back in the pastorate. He told God he was open to when and how God would lead him, but he also was cautious and wary about church ministry. For now a life of study, prayer, and reflection seemed the right thing to do. But was it really? Was he depressed? If so, what should he do about it?

6

Is There a Place for Me?

Candidating/Call

Dan slumped in his chair. Despondent and weary, he wondered where he and his wife, Nancy, would be in three months when he completed his interim position as pastor of First Church. This interim ministry had been a breath of fresh air after the disappointment and frustration he felt in his previous pastorate, but he could not help being anxious about the future.

Every place he had applied to be a teacher or pastor had rejected him—twenty in all—and even the university where he had applied for Ph.D. work had turned him down. At age fifty-four, he knew many churches would not consider him for a pastoral position, but he felt he had much to give and wanted to serve the Lord somewhere. In three months he would be out of a job, and his military pension was not enough to live on. Why was God silent?

Dan had entered pastoral ministry after twenty-three years in the military, sixteen of those as a chaplain. Even in the armed forces he had always thought of himself as a pastor in uniform. His experience as a military chaplain was quite extensive and varied. During his tenure as a military chaplain, he and Nancy and their three children had lived in several cities in the U.S. and abroad—at one time Dan had ministered to the military in Vietnam. In the chaplaincy he had especially enjoyed the pastoral aspects of ministry: counseling individuals, helping couples in marital distress, and preaching and teaching the Word of God. But the military bureaucracy and working with chaplains with different viewpoints from his was another matter. He was especially frustrated with the younger chaplains. Their theology, program emphasis, and ministry style were not to his liking.

While he looked back on his chaplaincy years as having many occasions of authentic ministry, he also struggled with reservations that the chaplaincy was "subsidized religion." In communities where local churches had good ministry to the military people, he wondered even more about the proper place of the military chaplain, especially when many stateside bases had a large chaplain corp.

Therefore, when he did not receive the necessary promotion to remain in the service, he was not too disappointed. His growing frustration with the chaplaincy and his yearning to settle down and work with a local church combined to mitigate his sense of failure at not receiving the promotion. He had served a two-year stint on a church staff before becoming a chaplain, and this had given him a good perspective on church and pastoral ministry.

So Dan left the military with a strong sense of God's leading to a new place of ministry, either teaching or pastoring. Without a Ph.D., Dan considered teaching in a Christian high school, knowing that his B.S. and M.Div. degrees were sufficient credentials in that context, but nothing opened up for him. He was interested in teaching biblical studies along with history or algebra. At the same time he was also looking for pastoral positions in his mainline denomination.

In the process of looking for a church, he was turned down by eight churches and withdrew his name from consideration in a ninth church. As he prepared to go to an interview at a church where he was being considered for the position of associate pastor, he was reading from Ephesians and took special note of Ephesians 5:17: "Don't be vague but firmly grasp what you know to be the will of the Lord" (PHILLIPS). He realized that in his years as a military chaplain he was in effect an associate pastor, and he knew he wanted no more of that, so he "firmly grasped" what he knew to be the will of God and canceled the interview.

On that very day he sensed God speaking to him from Psalm 114:7–8: "Dance, O earth, at the presence of the Lord, at the presence of the God of Jacob, who turned the rock into a pool of water, the granite cliff into a fountain" (NEB). If God could bring water from a rock, he could move in the hard hearts of people; Dan wanted to be part of that by having a pastorate of his own. Nancy set the psalmist's words to music in a rollicking chorus, and they waited expectantly on the leading of God.

Two weeks later as Dan prepared to go to an interview with a pastoral search committee from a church in a different mainline denomination from his own (the contact having come through a friend), another verse from Psalms spoke deeply to him: "Uphold me according to thy promise, that I may live, and let me not be put to shame in my hope!" (Ps. 119:116 RSV). God knew his hopes for a responsive congregation, and he knew he could trust God with his future and his transition from the military chaplaincy to civilian church life. With joy and confidence he went to interview with the search committee of The Village Church.

He and the committee hit if off immediately. They quickly extended a call to him to be their pastor, and he happily accepted. His call to the church paved the way for his honorable discharge from the military, and a few months later

Dan, Nancy, and their high school age son settled into their new home.

At one time The Village Church had been federated with a church of another denomination and was composed of people with diverse theological viewpoints, from very conservative to very liberal. When conflict arose over church structure, a group of the more liberal ones left the church and formed The Village Church. Later the original group that remained when the liberals left split again, so there were now three churches all within one mile of each other in a rural town of two thousand.

When Dan came, membership was around eighty, and average Sunday attendance in worship was forty-five. Few young or middle-aged people belonged to the church; most of the congregation were older people, and there were many widows. Young families visited the church from time to time but seldom returned.

Since The Village Church was affiliated with a denomination other than the one where Dan had his standing, he sought and received permission from his own denomination to be a pastor with this group. The only concern expressed by his denomination was the low salary being offered, but with his wife planning to work and his military pension, money was not a significant issue for Dan.

Aware that for the past twenty-five years The Village Church had not had a pastor stay more than four years, Dan made a commitment within himself to be a long-term pastor to the church. After being in the church for a few months he was convinced it would take at least ten years to turn things around. He set his sights on eight goals to be realized over the next ten to fifteen years of his ministry in the church:

1. To see the Lord Jesus Christ glorified in the town
2. To see all the Christian churches in town built up and growing

3. To double the Sunday worship attendance in five years
4. To triple the Sunday worship attendance of people between age twelve and forty in five years
5. To begin a Sunday school at a separate time from worship within three years
6. To begin a discipling class for mature believers within a few months
7. To see two people enter Christian ministry through the influence of the church
8. To learn more of God's love, joy, and humility

Within eight months of his arrival at the church, he translated these goals into four steps and proposed these to the deacons. Dan outlined the four steps on a large sheet of newsprint, drawing a baseball diamond for the four measurable objectives:

First base. I want to see genuine conversions to the Lord Jesus Christ and evidence that our people believe that the Bible and congregational worship are important.
Second base. I want to have sufficient children, adults, and interest to begin a Sunday school.
Third base. I want to have a mature and theologically alert group of leaders. (*Note:* On the newsprint Dan left this base blank, telling the deacons he would speak about it at a later date. He had it in his notes to present when there was opportunity. It is included here for the reader.)
Home plate. I want to see a strong and mature fellowship that after I'm gone will seek a pastor who shares my theological convictions. Such a congregation will possess individuals committed enough to pay a handsome salary to a man in his thirties. And finally I want to see one third of our total budget going towards mission endeavors at home and abroad that help the needy and spread the good news of Jesus Christ.

After he laid out these objectives, no one said anything for a long time. Finally one of the deacons suggested that the Sunday school could become first base. Dan quickly countered that since the Sunday school would require people who have a warm and meaningful relationship with the Lord Jesus, conversions should precede its establishment. After his comment, nothing more was said by any of the deacons.

Before Dan came to The Village Church, he felt excited about ministry in the church. He felt he would be able to energetically live out the dream that had been nourished in his heart for some time. It would be the kind of work he had longed to do as a chaplain, and he would not have to continually check his ideas and programs with several other unenthusiastic chaplains.

But a few weeks after arriving at the church, Dan concluded the church was in danger of dying. The church had only fifteen members under age forty and only eight of them attended with regularity. Dan's disappointment and concern deepened as the months went on. Four of the eight members under age forty who regularly attended the church stopped coming and were not going to church anywhere. Few men attended the church, in part due to the volunteer fire department in town holding weekly drills during the Sunday worship hour. On one occasion the wife of a fireman told Nancy that in their family if the son misbehaved during the week, he had to come to church with her, but if he was good, he could go to fire drill with his father on Sunday. Such a low view of church seemed entrenched in the community. The townspeople were friendly toward him but had little interest in spiritual matters. Privacy and independence were prized over religious beliefs and practices.

In one home visit to someone in the church, Dan asked the woman how things were going in her walk with God. She responded tartly, "That's none of your business!" He was stunned because he thought that was indeed his business. He was also discouraged over the liberal views of many people in the denomination to which the church belonged, especially their views on homosexuality.

Dan and Nancy made concerted efforts to get acquainted with other Christians in town and encourage them to become part of The Village Church. Most of these people attended churches in other towns, however, and although they enjoyed Christian fellowship and social activities with Dan and Nancy, they did not want to leave their churches to come to The Village Church. Dan and Nancy understood this but were disappointed that they did not have the support of these people in their ministry.

After some thought, Dan decided to implement an Evangelism Explosion program. He was convinced that new converts were the only way to build up a strong church with mature believers. The program was a complete failure. Few people were willing to participate, and those who did found the people they interviewed totally resistant to talking about the Christian faith.

Dan talked with the church leaders about setting up a membership class for the few new people who did visit the church, but the idea was rejected on the grounds that too many requirements would discourage new people from wanting to be members. The deacons occasionally asked townspeople who never came to church to serve as greeters at the church on Sundays as a way of getting new people interested in the church. But many of these people would not even stay for the worship service after their greeting duties were over.

In his second year at The Village Church, Dan began to grapple with fear, a gnawing fear that in spite of his best efforts the church wasn't going to make it. He would not succeed in turning this dying little church around. Dan decided to attend a church growth conference. The speaker listed the qualities of growing churches: a dynamic pastor, well-motivated laity, church programs of sufficient size to serve the expectations of people, people who think and behave alike, effective evangelistic outreach, the priority of salvation, evangelism, and missions in the church budget. Not one of the criteria described him or The Village Church. Dan's discouragement and frustration deepened.

A few months later Dan enjoyed a temporary bright spot. He attended another conference in which a prominent pastor and his wife talked about success in ministry. He was uplifted as this couple talked about success in biblical terms. He wrote in his date book their seven criteria for measuring success: faithfulness, service, loving God, believing, praying, holiness, and a positive and encouraging attitude. Perhaps he was not a failure after all, Dan thought, for these were all qualities he emulated or pursued.

His encouragement, however, was short-lived. One month later criticism of Dan began to surface from people in the church. Some said they felt scolded by his preaching. Others said he talked too much about obedience to God. The deacons said he was too judgmental and rigid.

Dan worked hard to prepare good sermons on the grace and redemptive work of God and was especially hurt by these criticisms. He knew he never mentioned judgment without emphasizing grace. Dan was not fully aware how lonely, disappointed, and angry he was becoming. A fellow minister and good friend did see this and encouraged him to seek a pastoral counselor, which he did. For the next four months Dan dealt with his thoughts and feelings under the guidance of a counselor.

Dan was an only child. His parents had divorced, and he lived with his mother, who married again and had several children with her second husband. Dan was driven to achieve, and his family setting taught him not to express his feelings. In the counseling sessions, Dan's counselor frequently asked him about his feelings. That exasperated Dan because he thought feelings were irrelevant even if they could be identified. But as the counseling progressed, he began to realize that he had intense feelings of anger, frustration, and disappointment, and he gradually came to see that not admitting to these feelings led to depression. As he came to understand his feelings, he gained some insight into his relationship with the people in church. On one occasion he said to the counselor, "I think I'm beginning to live again."

At one point during the counseling, a time of particular despair, he had a dream that was unusual and intense, and that he remembered vividly. In the dream his oldest son, Dannie Jr., was three or four years old and had been diagnosed as having an unspecified terminal disease. Dan was the only parent taking care of him. One day a coffin appeared at the door and came into the room. Dan was aware that he was to kill Dannie and put him in the coffin. "No way!" Dan shouted. "I will fight for my son's life and care for him until he draws his last breath. We are bound to each other, and I'm not giving up until the end!" When he awoke from the dream, he was relieved to remind himself that it was "only a dream" and his son Dannie was a healthy twenty-five-year-old.

Reflecting on the dream, Dan thought that Dannie represented The Village Church, which needed to die and be buried, but he wanted to fight for it and make it live. He felt bonded to the church by the call of God. The pastoral counselor raised another interpretation: In the dream Dannie represented Dan himself, whose name as a child was Dannie, and that he was slowly dying inside. Dan admitted that his playfulness, creativity, joy, and childlike sensitivity were all slowly dying. The counselor felt it was Dan's adult side that was roused to defend the part of him that was dying. Either way, Dan came to a conclusion: There was no hope of him having a satisfying ministry at The Village Church. When he acknowledged this, he felt angry—at himself, at people, at God, at nothing at all.

He was angry over how things had turned out. There was a huge gap between his expectations and the results. How could God have led him to such an unproductive place? He was sure God had led him to The Village Church, but had he been mistaken? Was he a failure? Did God care? At times Dan felt he was not adequate to run a car wash let alone a church. Even the pastoral counselor who had been so helpful saw him as a rigid person, closed to others, and with strong inner defenses.

Dan was aware that when he was around people, they seemed uncomfortable. It was hard for him to make small talk. People said he was too serious and did not smile enough. His response was "I want to go somewhere where my ministry does not depend on my smile! When teaching or preaching, content is first, people are second." But he knew not everyone saw it this way, and so they were uncomfortable around him. One part of him said this was not his problem, but another part wanted to be accepted by everyone.

Dan knew that he cared about people, cared deeply about their souls. "I accept people," he said, "but they don't feel it. On the other hand, if people feel guilty around me, it's probably because they are, and they ought to face up to it!" He wondered how he could hold up the standard of God's Word and at the same time accept people where they were. He confided to a friend that he "was not a smooth person that people like to be around," and that he often viewed people as an interruption. Left to himself he would rather study or work in the garden, but God had called him into Christian ministry, and he had a strong sense of the presence and guidance of God despite his feelings of disappointment and frustration.

By the end of his third year at The Village Church, Dan knew he had to leave. "I didn't want it to end this way," he confided to Nancy, "but I am forced to the bitter conclusion that there is absolutely no hope in our remaining here."

He wrote his letter of resignation and mailed it to the congregation.

The time has come for me to announce my resignation as your pastor. This has been a very difficult and agonizing decision for me to reach. But I have very reluctantly come to the conclusion that there is only a very limited place for me to minister here. When I first came three years ago it seemed clear to me that my first task was to build up a new base of committed membership, and in that endeavor I have singularly failed. Nor do I foresee any positive change while I remain here. For instance, our average attendance at worship, which I feel is a very important sign of congregational health, continues to slide.

Further, it appears to me that there is very little interest in serving on committees through which much of the work of the church is accomplished. Each December the Nominations Committee has a terrible time in getting our people to serve. Thus, we have been required to combine committees and to offer positions to non-members who are willing to serve. Our low level of giving to the ministry here is another indicator that my leadership has not worked well.

Personally, you have been courteous, tolerant and gracious toward me. I am thankful for the limited opportunity that I have been granted to minister to some of you. I am grateful that you have received me warmly. Yet I feel that my message has not been well received. With great regret I conclude that it is time for the church to look for another pastor who could better minister to your needs.

That week only four people responded in person to the letter. A few more expressed regret but not surprise when the letter was read at church the following Sunday. Most of the congregation seemed relieved.

Dan and Nancy spent much time talking about their situation. Nancy was as hurt and angry over what had happened as Dan was. Dan wished she had someone like his pastoral counselor to talk to, but she preferred to work through it on her own. She had a good outlet in her teaching job, but Dan knew she felt insecure about their future. His military pension and her salary were not enough for them to live on.

During this time Dan wrote the following in private correspondence:

> Looking back, I see a mismatch between me and The Village Church from the beginning. I am sure I answered God's call by going to the church. I thought it was exactly what I wanted. But God's guidance is something of a mystery. It must in the long run serve to bring him glory.
>
> So I leave with a profound sense of sadness. I tried to bring the message of God as I understand it, and it was declined. The people who heard it shoulder their own responsibility. I did not see much response, and therefore I feel they let me down. How did *I* get involved? It is God's message, and the hearers are responsible to him, not to me. That truth works for my head but not my stomach. My gut keeps score. It is the death of my dream. A word or smile from God would help at this point.

As Dan prepared to leave The Village Church, a church in a nearby community asked if he would be their interim pastor for a year. Dan jumped at the opportunity.

Now Dan's year as interim pastor was drawing to a close. It had been a good year working with committed and mature leaders and a responsive congregation. He was encouraged, and his vision was being renewed, but the pain of his three years at The Village Church was not completely gone.

Out of all the churches where he had sent his dossier, only one church was still considering him. This church needed an associate pastor with responsibilities for pastoral care. Dan was not sure the job description suited his gifts, and he wondered how he would fit on a large pastoral staff. He wondered if there was more disappointment ahead. He wondered, *Is there a place for me?*

7

We Need More Money

Money Problems

Ben and Holly had a quiet moment to talk. Their two younger children were down for their afternoon naps, and Todd, their oldest child, was away at school.

Once again they reviewed their options. They had talked about their finances so much before that they were tired of the subject, but tonight would be the annual meeting of the church. The congregation's decision about Ben's salary would guide their decision regarding whether Ben would resign from the church and seek a better paying job or continue as pastor of Bethel Baptist Church. They wanted to stay with the church, but they had long ago learned that what they wanted was not always what they got.

Ben felt called to be a pastor and had felt called in high school. Holly supported him and enjoyed the ministry with him. They met at seminary, and both were seminary graduates. After seminary they planned to go overseas to minister with an English-speaking congregation in another culture, but they first wanted to gain church experience in the

U.S. So Ben eagerly accepted a call to a Baptist church where he would serve as an assistant pastor with particular responsibility for youth.

Then Todd was born, and that changed everything. He was multiple-handicapped and had hydroencephalitis. Not only did their plans for overseas ministry change, but finances became a problem. Holly needed to stay home to care for Todd, and so could no longer continue her career as a school teacher. Ben's salary at the church was not even adequate for the two of them, let alone to handle the expenses of a handicapped baby.

As they now discussed the church meeting coming that night, however, money was not the only factor influencing their decision. Health care and adequate schooling for Todd were paramount in their minds. Leaving the ministry would mean a change of health insurance carriers, since the Baptist General Conference provided their insurance. It was available only to full-time pastors and church workers in the denomination.

The social worker who assisted them from time to time had indicated that obtaining other medical insurance would be a problem if they ever let their current coverage lapse. Medicaid helped to cover some expenses, but it was not sufficient for the treatment and care Todd needed in his special education classes; their health insurance covered the rest of the expenses.

Ben and Holly were in their mid-thirties. Bethel Baptist Church was the third church they had served. Sunday attendance was around one hundred, comprised mostly of older people who were conservative both in theology and financial management. They took great pride in the church building and had spent over one hundred thousand dollars the last three years remodeling it. Meanwhile they only paid Ben a yearly salary of twenty thousand dollars plus health insurance and retirement. From that salary, Ben had to pay rent, since the church did not own a parsonage. The church had sold its parsonage a number of years ago when the pastor at that time wanted to obtain his own house. The money from the parsonage sale had helped this pastor with the purchase of his own home. Some people in the church still resented the decision to sell the parsonage and help that pastor, and they had vowed to be more careful in the future with how they compensated their pastors. Ben knew this affected how they felt about his financial situation.

Ben's salary was barely enough for his family of five to live on. At one point he obtained a part-time job as a security guard to supplement his income, but church leaders made it clear they wanted him to drop the position and serve the church exclusively. Ben discussed his needs with them, but they did not offer him more money. He did, however, quit the part-time job—partly out of respect for the wishes of the church and partly out of a desire to be home in the evenings to help Holly with the children, especially with Todd.

Although Ben and Holly loved the people of Bethel Baptist Church and saw them as essentially good people, they were occasionally frustrated over the attitude they sensed in many members. Most had paid for their homes long ago. Even though many talked about their limited retirement incomes, they could afford to take vacation trips each year. Some even spent the entire winter in the South. They could buy new cars every few years. In contrast, Ben and Holly lived in a small, three-bedroom apartment and had never driven anything but "rust buckets."

None of the churches Ben served had paid well, but at least the attitude of the people in the first two churches reflected more concern for the well-being of Ben's family. In fact, people in the other churches apologized for not being able to do more. But in Bethel Church people seemed to think Ben and Holly were the problem. The leaders told Ben they thought he and Holly had "a problem managing money," and suggested they get advice from a financial counselor. That hurt.

Both Ben and Holly had educational loans they were repaying. In addition they owed the government seven thousand dollars. An agency had mistakenly given them that amount for Todd's care, and now Ben and Holly were in the process of paying it back. But this government money was not something they had intentionally taken as a loan; it was clearly a mistake of the government. Although when the error was found, the money had already been spent for Todd's care, Ben agreed to pay it back—even though some friends suggested he get a lawyer and fight it.

Their combined educational loans of seventeen thousand dollars required them to pay two hundred dollars a month for ten years. The payment took over 10 percent of their salary, and this seemed to be what bothered some of the older people in the congregation, who did not believe people should take out loans for education. Ben and Holly did not see how they would have gotten their education without borrowing money. Both had gone to state schools for their undergraduate education, where tuition was less than private schools, so their only borrowing had come while in seminary. Many couples they knew had far greater loans. When they borrowed the money, they did not think it would be difficult to pay it back on time. In fact, with both of them working they anticipated paying off the loans early so they could go overseas five years after graduation, knowing that no mission agency would allow them to go to the field with indebtedness. But they hadn't planned on Todd's disabilities.

When they first went to Bethel Baptist Church, which was located in the Chicago area, they lived for a while with Ben's mother. They did this primarily to save money, but the arrangement was not entirely satisfactory, and they quickly saw it as a short-term situation. Not only did both Ben and Holly find it awkward to be around his mother all the time, but the space they had for themselves and their children was only one and a half rooms.

When Ben and Holly were able to get their own apartment, the one they currently lived in, the rent, though good for the Chicago area, strained their modest income to the limit. Even though the apartment was small, Ben and Holly liked to entertain church people, regularly having others into their home for meals or meetings. On one occasion when some women were at the apartment for a meeting, however, one of them actually criticized Holly for having such a small place to entertain in.

Before Todd was born, Holly had feared giving birth to a handicapped child. At one point she said to Ben, "God will never give us more than we can handle, and he knows I will have a nervous breakdown if we have a handicapped child." Her brother had fathered a handicapped child. Her parents were not Christians, and Holly also prayed that the baby would be the means of their coming to faith (which in fact happened, but not for the reason Holly first prayed).

When Todd was born hydroencephalitic, Holly was shocked to the core. In the days following his birth, she felt like Job, and on more than one occasion she said she wanted to "curse God and die." Were it not that Ben was the youth pastor of the church and had to be at church services, Holly did not think she would have gone to church at all in the weeks following Todd's birth. She had taken good care of herself during the pregnancy, and she and Ben had given their lives to the service of God. It just didn't seem fair.

The church was very supportive of Ben and Holly when Todd was born. Todd was the first baby born to one of their pastors in many years, and the people were excited about it. The women gave several generous baby showers during the pregnancy. News of Todd's disabilities caused tears to abound throughout the congregation, and the people surrounded Ben and Holly with love, prayers, and support. One woman even insisted on staying with Todd one day a week when he first came home from the hospital so Holly could have a day off.

In addition to being hydroencephalitic, Todd "failed to thrive." He was in and out of the hospital many times during his first few months of life. When he was nine months old, he had a gastrostomy tube inserted into his stomach for feeding. At the time, doctors doubted he would live beyond a few more days, but he did. The membrane around his brain was no thicker than tissue paper because of being so compressed by water. He was later diagnosed as being legally blind, and there was doubt whether he was educable.

Holly handled her grief primarily through anger, describing her feelings as "a rage like a cancer eating me up." Ben handled his pain by throwing himself into the work of the church. At first Holly's anger frightened Ben. He feared she was turning away from God. He, on the other hand, was desperately seeking God and felt driven to him. So for a short time there was tension between them, but before long love and open communication brought them together in a deeper level of understanding.

Holly's anger helped her not to be overcome with sorrow, and enabled her to channel her energy to advocate for proper care for Todd. The institutions of society that Ben and Holly thought would be there for them—medical care, social welfare, and education—were at times not there. Holly's anger forced decisions to be made in Todd's interest that might not otherwise have happened.

It took most of the first year after Todd was born for Holly to get over her intense anger. She read a book by the mother of a child who died of cancer. The mother prayed for healing for the child, but it did not happen (not in the earthly sense at least). Holly felt intensely angry at God for letting something like this happen to innocent children. But she was suddenly aware that God was also angry at what happened to that child and what happened to Todd. God was angry at sin and the effect of sin on humankind. That's why he sent Jesus. Jesus not only identified with suffering people and comforted those who were in agony, but he took action at the cross to abolish sin and its effects forever. These truths burned a new path into her soul. For the first time she began to feel that God *shared* the anger she felt. Slowly, the anger within her began to dissolve in tears.

Even though their first church was supportive of Ben and Holly in many ways, it was also having trouble with its own finances. Ben was the first youth pastor the church had ever hired. In fact, it was the first time they had ever had a second minister on staff. So even though the congregation wanted to pay Ben more, the money just wasn't there. Ben felt he needed to get a church where he could exercise all his gifts in the broad aspects of pastoral ministry, so he sought a call elsewhere. He and Holly had concluded that they did not need to go overseas to fulfill his call to pastoral ministry. Todd's situation had effectively closed the door for overseas ministry.

In a short time Ben received a call to pastor a Baptist General Conference church in rural Illinois, about three hundred miles from Chicago. So three years after Ben and Holly came to their first church and two years after Todd was born, they said their good-byes on Easter Sunday. Holly told the congregation, "I have learned through Todd's condition that we serve God because he is God, not because he does nice things for us."

The ministry in their second church went well. Like the first church, the people of this church surrounded them with love and support during some anxious moments. Holly became pregnant and soon suffered a miscarriage. She conceived again. But this time she gave birth to a normal, healthy girl whom they named Kristy.

Ben went to this church expecting to stay for a long time, but low salary and inadequate medical facilities nearby to care for Todd became important issues. After talking openly with the leaders of the church and praying over the course of several months with the whole congregation about what to do, the congregation and Ben and Holly agreed it would be best if they returned to the Chicago area where Todd could get the medical treatment and schooling he needed. So after a little more than two years in the church, Ben received a call from Bethel Baptist Church to be their pastor, and he, Holly, Todd, and Kristy moved back to the Chicago area.

Todd was now four years old. In addition to the home care provided by Holly and Ben, a visiting nurse came to the house several times a week. Holly also took Todd to physical therapy, speech therapy, and special education classes several times a week. With the move, Todd was able to begin special education classes in a full-day program five days a week. Even though he had been diagnosed earlier as being uneducable, he was showing signs of the ability to learn and do some things for himself. Ben and Holly thought it was important for Todd to get all the professional help he could in the educational system, and once again their advocacy skills were brought to the fore as they confronted systems reluctant to help.

In their second year at Bethel church, Holly gave birth to their second son, Lee. When Lee was born, some people in the church hinted that it was time Ben and Holly stopped having children. It was too much of a risk for them, people said, and children were a big expense. This was another reason why the church leaders suggested Ben get some financial counseling.

Such advice seemed ironic to Ben and Holly since several of the church people came from large families and had large families themselves. Ben and Holly concluded that having children was their decision with the Lord and no one else's. It did not help, however, that Lee cried a great deal and was very demanding, leaving Holly tired much of the time and unable to be active in the church. People said they understood, but Holly also got the feeling that some people expected her to do more.

Another point of tension with church leaders was Ben's

distance from church. The commute from the apartment to the church building was ten miles through heavy traffic, but Ben could not afford to rent an apartment closer to the church. Church members wanted Ben and Holly to live nearer the church and did not understand why the salary they paid Ben would not allow for that.

In preparation for the annual meeting, Ben had talked with the church leaders about his financial situation. He had gone over every detail of the family budget with them, including rent, educational loans, and the personal costs for caring for Todd that Medicaid and insurance did not cover.

The numbers surprised some of the leaders, and they said they wanted to see the church increase the salary, but they weren't sure the church could afford it. Others frowned at Ben being so forthright about such a private matter. A few thought Ben's action was another indicator that he could not manage money and wanted others to do it for him. Ben thought it was quite clear that twenty thousand dollars a year was not sufficient for a family of five to live on in the Chicago area—not in the 1990s and especially not with a handicapped child needing costly care. He said the church should put more effort into improving his salary than redecorating the building. That comment upset a few people, but Ben had done what he thought was right, and he had done it in a way he thought honored the Lord. Now it was up to the church.

So in their quiet apartment after lunch, Ben and Holly talked. Holly said reflectively, "God is in charge of everything, isn't he? And he gives us grace each day for what we need. For a long time I demanded answers from God, but now I just want to obey and trust him for everything."

Ben was silent for awhile, and then said, "Yes, you're right. And I'm encouraged in my own faith to hear you say it. I don't know how we would have survived what we have without the Lord. I wish I knew what the congregation was going to decide tonight. We need more money. What should we do if the church says no?"

103

8

Was Ted Unfair?

Staff Relationships/Gender Issues

$\mathcal{S}$usan felt a deep ache in her soul. No matter how much she went over the incident in the staff meeting she could not get over the hurt. She doubted that she could ever trust Ted again.

At the weekly staff meeting of First Presbyterian Church three weeks ago, Ted "dumped" on Susan. Ted, the senior minister, had reminded the other ministers of an upcoming presbytery meeting. Susan, one of three ordained associates, said she had a wedding to perform in the church that day and would miss the presbytery meeting. Ted exploded, accusing her of not taking seriously her responsibility to the presbytery. Susan was shocked at the intensity of Ted's words and feelings. She thought his behavior was unfair since the wedding had been scheduled through the regular procedures of the church—and it was her turn to officiate at a wedding.

After the meeting Susan went immediately to her office, closed the door, and cried. She felt it was unfair for Ted to accuse her of not doing her job well. *I work for the church fifty to sixty hours a week,* she thought, *and this is what I get. And Ted is gone almost half the time to this meeting and that board. He gets the whole summer off, too; none of the rest of us gets that kind of perk!* Susan was also irked that the other two associate ministers had conflicts that prevented them from attending the presbytery meeting, but he said nothing to them. Most of all she felt humiliated to be spoken to in such a demeaning manner in front of the rest of the staff (six other support staff were also at the meeting).

As Susan sat in her office in tears reflecting on what had happened, Ted came to the office and presented in writing three concerns he had about her. Ted's first concern was the wedding incident just addressed in the staff meeting. The second issue concerned a time she had not rescheduled a deacons meeting in order to arrive on time at a presbytery retreat. Ted had canceled his meeting with the session so he could attend the retreat, but Susan had found it difficult to arrange alternative meetings for the deacons because of the large number, sixty-five in all, for whom she was responsible. Several weeks before the retreat she sent a memo to Ted informing him she would be late to the retreat, but he said nothing about it until now. The third issue arose at a staff meeting, after Ted learned that Susan would be attending a conference he also was planning to attend. Ted expressed surprise that Susan would attend this conference and suggested it would be best if they were not gone from the church at the same time. Conference organizers had asked her to lead one of the sessions, however, so she had to go. In the end, Susan and Ted both attended the meeting. *Is he jealous that they asked me to speak and not him?* she wondered.

When he brought his concerns to her, he spoke tersely, adding that was his "one-minute manager style." She asked if he had one minute to praise her for anything. He looked at her with surprise but said nothing. Then he reminded her that the pastor of the church she worked in for nine years before coming to First Presbyterian Church had wanted to get rid of her. Susan responded that what happened then had no relevance to the situation now. She had been at First Presbyterian Church for eleven years now and was handling enormous responsibilities, including commitment to the presbytery. Ted said he brought up the past to raise the question of whether she was doing something that caused men to respond as he had just done in the meeting. This statement stunned her. It was as though Ted was saying, "It's your fault that I exploded and was demeaning to you." But she did not say what she was thinking.

Over the next few days, however, Susan thought a great deal about what had happened. She tried to understand what might have caused Ted to say what he did. He had been totally supportive of her as a woman in ministry and had encouraged her to use her gifts and take on heavy responsibilities in the church. But she also knew he was strongly committed to the PCUSA, and so presbytery meetings had high priority for him. He was especially concerned that evangelicals like him and Susan be visible, vocal, and supportive of the presbytery. She knew her commitment was not as strong as his, but she was by no means unsupportive or disloyal. At times she wondered if Ted was not a bit irrational about his zeal to be present at presbytery meetings, but she also knew he hoped to run for denominational office someday, so it was understandable that he would give higher priority to presbytery meetings than she would.

Susan also wondered how much Ted's situation at home might be causing him stress. A seriously ill child had drained him of energy. Ted's wife had begun to develop her gifts and abilities in ways that took her out of the home pursuing her professional career. While Ted was supportive of this, it demanded adjustments on his part. Susan wondered if Ted was frustrated over these changing roles, and he was taking his frustration out on her. She knew she was engaging in pure speculation. If she was doing something that annoyed Ted, she was willing to take responsibility for it.

Susan knew she was often assertive. *But what's wrong with that?* she thought. *Men are assertive and are expected to be, but when women exert strong and confident leadership, they are often seen as "coming on too strong."* She described herself as a self-starter but also was a team player well-suited for a staff position. She enjoyed her work and felt privileged to serve the Lord for twenty years in church ministry.

Occasionally she talked with Cindy, one of the other full-time ordained ministers on the staff, about how their roles as women ministers seemed to threaten the male ministers as well as numerous people in the church. They observed that on the one hand they were encouraged and supported, but on the other hand they were not as free to exercise their gifts as men were and had to be careful not to overstep certain bounds. In their view, no such restrictions were placed on men.

Susan and Cindy nevertheless encouraged each other to be cheerful and faithful in carrying out their ministries. Others saw them as confident and competent in their work, but Susan and Cindy felt at times they got less respect than men in ministry positions.

In light of the incident in the staff meeting, Susan wondered about her future in the church. Ted's comment about the pastor in her former church wanting to get rid of her troubled her. *Does Ted want to get rid of me?* she wondered.

As a single woman, she had no one else to depend on for her livelihood. Although she felt sure she could find a position in another church if necessary, she did not want to leave First Presbyterian Church. She had often said to her friends, "Men forgive each other easily, but they get rid of women who give them problems." She did not want that to happen to her, so as much as it angered her—she felt it was unfair treatment by Ted in the first place that had brought her to this point and she did not want anything to hinder her free involvement in ministry—she resolved to be careful about what she said and did in the future.

Ted's outburst had so shaken Susan that she found herself avoiding him in the days following the incident. She had lost respect for him and did not trust him. "I will not be vulnerable again," she said to a friend. "We were like a family, and Ted was like a brother to me, but now I've pulled back. I don't want to be hurt like that again."

In the days following Ted's outburst, he went out of his way to be nice to her. Susan was surprised and pleased when at the staff meeting the next week Ted said to the ten people assembled, "I'm sorry for the way the staff meeting went last week and for the way Susan got the brunt of my frustration." Susan did not know how to react, so she said nothing. Ted's comments sounded a bit forced to Susan, and she wondered if he was apologizing more because of the effect his outburst had on her and the staff than because he thought what he did was wrong.

As the days went on, Susan continued to reflect on what had happened. For her, the incident illustrated how men make women feel. First, women are often demeaned by men if they are confident and competent in their work, and second, when something goes wrong, men often make women feel it's their fault. She had received demeaning and unfair comments from Ted, but then he made her feel it was her fault.

She felt this kind of thinking and behaving characterized American society, and it was not that different in the church. There was too much to do for the work of God's kingdom to be bogged down in these kinds of relationships, she thought, but in an imperfect and fallen world people say and do things that hurt others. *I'm not Miss Perfect myself,* she mused as she thought about her responsibility in the matter.

She still felt hurt, betrayed, angry, and disappointed. She knew it would be a long time before she would get over the overwhelming feeling of having to be cautious around Ted.

Despite Ted's apology she feared it would happen again. She and Ted had not talked about what had happened beyond their conversation immediately after the staff meeting. Until this happened, she and Ted could talk freely with each other about their responsibilities and ministries, but now there was a distance between them. Would it ever be like it used to be? What was her responsibility in making the situation and relationship better? What should Susan do?

9

Rob's Reflections on Spirituality

Spirituality

*R*ob sat in his office thinking about his spiritual pilgrimage. He had agreed to discuss with a friend the topic of spirituality in the life of the pastor, and his friend was due to arrive any minute.

Rob had always been a reflective person by nature. Even before he became a Christian and was called into pastoral ministry, he had always been religious. So he sometimes wondered if his spiritual pilgrimage was a reflection of his personality and the way he naturally viewed things, or was a direct result of God's providence in his life. Perhaps the two could not be separated, but he wasn't sure.

When Rob was in college at a private and prestigious secular school, he was searching for religious reality and meaning in life, so he majored in religious studies. After his study of Eastern religions, he established a daily pattern of doing transcendental meditation in the morning and evening. Most of the Christians he had known seemed phony to him. Their religion wasn't incorporated into their lives. His East-

ern religion friends seemed more humble and more genuine than the Christians he knew on campus. He was a quiet,
gentle, and reflective person who liked to visit chapels to
pray and think, so he saw himself fitting better into an Eastern religion than into Christianity, with its often frenetic
activity and what he perceived as a dichotomy between belief
and behavior.

During his sophomore year in college, one of his close
friends had a Christian friend who began to talk seriously
with Rob about the Christian faith. Although Rob was open
to listen, he had strong reservations. In addition to the seem-
ing phoniness of most Christians, he had trouble believing
in a God of grace. The idea of grace alone being the only
means by which a person could be in fellowship with God
seemed incongruous to Rob. Didn't he have to do something besides believe in what God had done for him through
the death of Christ on the cross? The grace Christians talked
about was too simple.

Eventually, however, through the persistent witness of
Christian students who took an interest in him, he embraced
the Christian faith and began a new journey in "practicing
the presence of God" as a Christian. The Christian friend
who had been witnessing to him continued to teach and
nurture him in the Christian faith. Also a nearby pastor of
an evangelical church that had an effective ministry to college students took Rob under his wing and discipled him.
Rob responded wholeheartedly.

His reflective nature did not change when he became a
Christian, but his focus did. Before he was a Christian, meditation was a means for producing a quiet inner life; now as
a Christian, meditation became the means of experiencing
God's presence, and Bible study became a vehicle for knowing God better and living for him in the world.

It was no surprise, then, to those who knew Rob well that
when he graduated from college two years after his Christian conversion he decided to become a staff member of

Campus Crusade for Christ, a parachurch ministry with a strong emphasis on evangelism and ministry to college students. Rob appreciated his experience with Christian leaders in his own college days, and he wanted to work with students who themselves needed Christian mentoring. After training for eight weeks over the summer, Rob began his Campus Crusade work at a large university in the Northeast. His devotional life continued to flourish. Bill Bright, the founder and leader of Campus Crusade, was fond of saying, "No Bible, no breakfast." Rob liked that emphasis and was delighted to be working at something that was enjoyable in the first place—talking to students about Jesus and nurturing Christians in the faith—and that placed such a strong emphasis on personal devotions and Bible study.

At one national meeting for Crusade staff, Rob met Cathy, another Crusade staff worker. He liked her spunk and outgoing personality, which complemented well his quiet nature. Romance blossomed, and they married two years later. Cathy was not happy in the ministry of Campus Crusade, and Rob began to consider the call of God to enter pastoral ministry. So when they married they made the decision to leave Crusade and go to seminary.

In the process of choosing a seminary, Rob did something quite out of character. Several people had encouraged him to attend a particular school, but he had chosen a different one. He was driving with Cathy to that seminary with all their belongings in the car, when he suddenly turned the car around and headed halfway across the country to the seminary recommended by his friends. His impulsive choice worked out well, and he was thankful for his seminary experience.

As a seminary student Rob's spiritual life continued to grow, although his spirituality took an academic turn. Understanding the biblical text was a newfound venture that excited him. His daily meeting with God was focused more on discovering biblical truth than on meditation, reflection, and prayer. When studying, he kept a list of questions he had and talked with friends and professors about his questions, which contributed to his growth in knowledge and to his spiritual life.

His practice of reading through the Bible in one year, however, slowed down to completing such reading in two and a half years. The keeping of a prayer journal, as he did during his Campus Crusade days, lapsed. He also found less time available for his accustomed one hour of daily prayer. Still he often went to the seminary chapel to spend time in quiet reflection and prayer. He was puzzled by student friends who complained about the difficulty of maintaining their spiritual lives in seminary. On the whole his spirituality was still intact.

The same could not be said for Cathy, however. The transition from full-time Crusade worker to full-time wife and provider was difficult for her. Five days a week she commuted one hour each way to work, and her coworkers were non-Christians. When she came home, she longed to spend time with Rob, but he was always studying. Cathy cried a lot that year. Rob was, admittedly, "selfish and even rude" with Cathy, but he could not understand why she was upset.

He especially could not understand Cathy's lack of spirituality, as he saw it. She did not spend much time in Bible reading or prayer. He felt he was partly to blame because it was his responsibility as the head of the house to see that her spiritual life went well. So he prayed that both he and Cathy would change. When nothing happened immediately, he wondered if God cared about them. Surely God was concerned about their spiritual walk, but he did not appear to be doing anything about it. Such thinking infrequently led to bouts of spiritual depression, and he would find himself pulling away from God.

While they were in seminary, Cathy sought counseling for help in career planning, and this led to marriage counseling, which greatly helped in stabilizing their relationship.

They gained insight into their different needs and ways of relating to God and found a new appreciation for one another as individuals before God. Rob did not feel as responsible for Cathy's spiritual well-being, and he was content to let her find her own way with God. He was also trying to spend more time with her.

Cathy began to find joy and meaning in a new career: counseling. She also felt less dependent on Rob for many things, including her spiritual well-being. They were different, that was for sure. She was outgoing, questioning, and open in her expression of doubts and uncertainties. He was quiet, trusting, reflective, and tended to keep his thoughts to himself. But they were making it together. They finished seminary in five years, with their marriage intact and with a growing relationship with God.

After completing seminary, Rob received a call to pastor a Presbyterian church affiliated with the PCUSA in a medium-sized city in the Northeast. He soon enjoyed being a pastor and was viewed by others as a godly man. But he found that maintaining one's spiritual life as a pastor is hard work. While he resisted seeing devotions as a requirement from God—"The Bible does not command that we have devotions," he would often say—he also knew he was the happiest, most content, and felt what he called "the most sublime joy" when he was reading the Bible and meditating on it in quiet before God.

It was during these devotional times that Rob would describe his spiritual experience as "being overwhelmed with a feeling of grace." This was important to him, since from his earliest days as a Christian he had trouble understanding the grace of God, and he knew that years later he was still having trouble with it.

In spite of working hard at his spiritual life, Rob confessed to a friend that he felt "much guilt much of the time." He never felt like he was as spiritual as he should be. "I don't give myself permission to relax much with my spiritual life," he said. Spirituality was serious business for Rob not only for his own relationship with God but for his functioning as a pastor. When he was walking with God as he wanted to, he was more patient with people, more sensitive and caring, ministering the grace of Christ to them. He was more relaxed and felt like a whole person.

When he was not maintaining his spiritual life, he felt cold and indifferent with people. He went through the motions with no feeling of grace but rather with a sense of being driven. So Rob was concerned about his spiritual life because it had direct impact on his pastoral duties, but he was quick to say, "My spiritual life is important because I'm a Christian, not just because I'm a pastor."

Rob found it hard to prepare sermons, and he thought that was curious. He was quick to stop what he was doing to pray about something that came to mind. Often when he was attending to pastoral or administrative duties in his office, he stopped what he was doing and went into the sanctuary for a time of meditation and prayer. It seemed natural and good. Sermon preparation, on the other hand, was mechanical. He followed a technical approach to exegesis and felt God's guidance was there in elucidating the text and giving him ideas on what to preach, but he seldom prayed during preparation. *Do other ministers do it this way?* he wondered.

He also wondered if other ministers procrastinated in preparing a sermon the way he did. Usually his sermons were done at the last minute, and although he occasionally felt a little anxious about this, he knew that advance preparation made him even more anxious. He was more ready to preach after just finishing a sermon than if he wrote it several days ahead of time. Comments he received from people in the church indicated they appreciated his preaching and were helped in their own spiritual walk by it. *Maybe praying about myself and not my sermons is the best approach,* he thought.

As Rob thought more about his spiritual life, he recalled

a deep point of spiritual depression, for both him and Cathy. It began six years earlier when Cathy's sister died of cancer, followed two years later by the death of this sister's husband from Lou Gehrig's Disease. Although the sister was nineteen years older than Cathy, Cathy had always enjoyed a close and affectionate relationship with her and her husband. Rob, too, had enjoyed the warmth of a close relationship to them. When the diseases were discovered, Rob and Cathy, along with scores of Christians, had prayed for their healing. Many people, including Rob and Cathy, had a strong sense that God would heal them, but the diseases did their ravaging work.

At the two funerals Rob looked at the children now left without a father or mother, the youngest of whom was still in high school, and he broke down and cried, wondering where God was. He had never felt such heaviness, such anger and disappointment with God. He could not understand how God could let this happen, and he did not want to be close to God. He found himself withdrawing from daily devotions. Some people in the church wanted to talk about the situation, but Rob could not. Cathy was even more upset than Rob, withdrawing completely from prayer.

After a time, Rob and Cathy began to experience healing from their anger towards God and their anguish over their family. Other Christians had seen their pain and had been in prayer for them. Months later a pastor friend told Rob he had been praying for him for a long time. Rob was humbled and thankful to know that God's faithful people were praying for him and Cathy without judging them, and he realized that God was indeed working in their lives. They came to view prayer less mechanistically and to acknowledge that God is both sovereign and good. Rob realized that God may not answer prayer as people want, but he gives his children grace to handle even the tragedies of life. Again for Rob, God's grace was both a blessing and an obstacle.

117

During that dark period, Rob spent three days at an Episcopal retreat center. The priests there take vows of celibacy and obedience, spend time in fellowship with each other and in reflective prayer, and offer retreats to others who desire to examine their own spiritual lives. Rob spent part of the time in conversation with the priests and in group prayer, and part of the time in private prayer and meditation. Through this experience he regained his individual discipline in prayer and meditation, and rediscovered the resources of grace present in other Christians. At the retreat center he felt God healing his wounded spirit.

Looking back on his spiritual pilgrimage, Rob was reminded of a continuing concern; he and Cathy seldom spent time together in Bible reading and prayer. They had tried many times, but it did not work for them. In fact, their personalities were so different that it only created tension. On the positive side, they had found freedom over the years supporting one another in their individual walks with God. Describing their approach to spirituality to a friend, Rob said, "We are each responsible adults before the Lord, and we encourage one another to grow with God."

His concern now was how they would teach their daughter, now three, about spiritual life. He and Cathy each prayed with her separately, but they didn't do it together. *What kind of a message is this sending to her?* he wondered.

Rob knew that spirituality was an ongoing process, not a static event. There had been many ups and downs along the way, and he knew there would be more. During his brief years as a pastor he had talked with enough ministers to know that nurturing the spiritual life was difficult for many of them. But it was not something they freely talked about with each other. In fact, Rob could not remember when a fellow minister ever raised the issue in private conversation with him or in a meeting of ministers. Rob was always the first one to bring it up.

He resolved to continue the disciplines of prayer and meditation that brought him such joy and contentment. He was content with his relationship to God and also eager to continue growing in his spiritual life. In fact, he could hardly wait until his friend arrived so they could talk about these things. He wished ministers were more willing to talk to each other about the spiritual side of their lives. He also wished his seminary professors and buddies had made it more of a focus of regular conversation. He wondered, *Why don't we?*

10

Can't We Worship Together and Be Happy?

Conflict

*C*harles drove to church thinking about the elders meeting scheduled for the following night. The only item on the agenda of this specially called meeting was to review the results of the survey the congregation had completed at the request of the elders on the subject of the style of worship and music for Community Church. Charles had just finished reviewing the results of the survey. Clearly the congregation was as divided as ever on worship style.

Once again Charles thought about the never-ending but usually low-level controversy over worship style during his six years as pastor of Community Church. *Isn't it ironic,* he thought, *that the subject of the Holy Spirit, who is supposed to be a unifying presence in the church, is so divisive?* He reflected on Ephesians 4:1–6:

> I urge you to live a life worthy of the calling you have received. Be completely humble and gentle; be patient, bear-

121

ing with one another in love. Make every effort to keep the unity of the Spirit through the bond of peace. There is one body and one Spirit—just as you were called to one hope when you were called—one Lord, one faith, one baptism; one God and Father of all, who is over all and through all and in all.

Charles wondered why they could not experience this reality and how much longer he could be the glue that held the disparate groups together. His mind wandered over the events of the past six years.

When Charles came to Community Church, it was deeply divided even then over the style of worship and type of music. Friends of Charles had advised him not to go to the church, but he felt God was leading and would bless the ministry. He had been a pastor for a little over twelve years before coming to Community Church, and as he evaluated his overall experience and his knowledge of this church, he thought he should accept the invitation from the congregation to be its pastor.

In his seminary days Charles had attended Community Church and had done his field education there. His wife, Grace, had also been active in the church. Both Charles and Grace knew the church well, having followed its development during the years they had worked in three other churches after he graduated from seminary. Those three were strong and healthy but not without the typical problems all churches face with various expectations and demands of parishioners. So Charles was not unfamiliar with controversy.

His previous church was composed of leaders in the high-tech industry who had high expectations for what the church should be and what the pastor should do. Although Charles got along with them well, it seemed the church wanted to be an "organizational church," as he called it, or a "program church" with something for everyone, rather than a church that emphasized preaching, teaching, and living the gospel in the world—the latter being the kind of church he felt he was best qualified to lead.

With this in mind, then, Charles and Grace felt God was leading them to Community Church. This meant leaving their denomination and coming to a church unaffiliated with any denomination. This wasn't difficult since the denomination they belonged to was loosely organized, and the polity of Community Church resembled churches in his denomination.

Community Church was located in a town of five thousand people in a seacoast community that relied heavily on tourism to support the local economy. The church traced its history to 1829 and was proud of its long tradition of worshiping and serving God in the community. At one time several churches in that part of town served various ethnic groups, but one by one these churches closed and joined forces, eventually becoming Community Church. Most church members were commercial fishermen; others were laborers in light industries or involved in the tourist trade.

The church was Baptist in theology but utilized a board of elders. The elders served under the authority of the congregation and had authority delegated to it by the congregation to oversee the programs and spiritual life of the church.

Just before Charles came, Community Church suffered a split, with one-third of the congregation leaving with the pastor who had been there for seven years. This pastor, whose name was Fred, had come to the church as a seminary student to work as a member of a two-person pastoral team with Bruce, who was a seminary professor and also worked part-time at the church. The church could not afford a full-time pastor, but Bruce and Fred served combined hours that equaled that of a full-time person.

Bruce had been the interim pastor of the church on a part-time basis at the time of Fred's coming. In the new arrangement Bruce and Fred would each have the title co-pastor. Fred would live in the parsonage, something the congregation wanted one of them to do, and Bruce already had his own home near the seminary. Fred was also to work with church committees, do pastoral visitation, and preach twice a month. Bruce would also preach twice a month, do pastoral counseling, and provide overall leadership and vision to the leaders, including Fred, and to the congregation.

Problems developed almost immediately between Fred and Bruce. Fred's theology and experience were charismatic. This was not the general stance of the church although a few individuals were open to the experience and had attended various pentecostal meetings. Bruce and the church leaders discussed Fred's position on this issue before Fred was hired. During the interview Fred said their doctrinal differences would not be a problem for him, nor would it be the focus of his preaching or teaching.

Once in the pulpit, however, Fred began immediately emphasizing the pentecostal experience. While some people were disturbed by this, others expressed their delight. Bruce talked with Fred about this in private on several occasions, calling attention to the statements Fred made prior to coming to the church and the potential divisiveness of the teaching. Fred said he felt he should continue his emphasis because God was leading him to minister in this way. He also noted the favorable response from some church members.

Fred also began to make decisions about programs and policies of the church without consulting with Bruce and only occasionally with the elders. Several of the elders welcomed this as strong leadership from Fred, saying this was what the church needed to grow.

Although Bruce was dissatisfied with his relationship with Fred and was concerned about Fred's preaching emphasis and style of leadership, he increasingly observed that the people and some of the elders welcomed Fred's leadership and charismatic emphasis. Discussions on the topic between

Bruce and Fred usually left Bruce frustrated. He felt there was no productive way to get at the issues since Fred typically responded that God led him to do what he did. Bruce began to pull back and question whether the congregation in general wanted a more charismatic style of worship than he was comfortable with. Nevertheless he committed himself to work with Fred and try to minister to the people who had called them both to serve as co-pastors.

After working together for over a year, things came to a head between Bruce and Fred when two elders left the church with their families. They had reservations about the team ministry from the beginning. These elders had recently begun to express doubts to various people in the church about Fred's emphasis in ministry and worship and about how the team ministry was functioning.

When Fred heard about these conversations, he went—without consulting Bruce—to these two elders and told them that after praying and fasting he felt led by God to ask them to seek a church home elsewhere, since they would be resistant to his ministry. The two men immediately resigned their positions as elders and left the church. When Bruce learned about the incident two weeks later, he immediately confronted Fred. Fred gave his usual response: God had led him to do what he did so the church could "put the past behind and begin to grow."

At that point, Bruce went to the elders and requested they call a special congregational meeting. He asked for the agenda to include discussion on (1) the different theological emphases he and Fred had (his being Reformed and Fred's being charismatic); (2) how their theological understandings guided their individual approaches to ministry and decision making; and (3) which style of ministry and worship the congregation wanted.

The remaining four elders indicated they felt some measure of relief with the two families leaving. They also stated they thought the congregation in general was pleased with

Fred's ministry and the charismatic elements he had introduced to the worship service. Out of respect for Bruce, however, they agreed to call a congregational meeting to discuss the issues.

At the congregational meeting, most of the active members were present. The plan called for Bruce to introduce the topic at hand as outlined on the agenda he drew up with the elders, but when the moderator called the meeting to order, Fred asked for the privilege of speaking first. This was granted, and Fred stood to announce that he had been able to secure financial support from several churches and individuals as a home missionary, so if the church wanted him to serve as full-time pastor while continuing his seminary studies on a part-time basis, that would be possible. When Fred finished speaking, excited talking and even some applause spontaneously broke out among the members.

The moderator turned to Bruce and asked if he had anything to say. Bruce stood and offered to resign if the church wanted to accept Fred's offer. His resignation was accepted unanimously and with appreciation for his ministry. The congregation then voted Fred in as the new pastor on a full-time basis. At that point Bruce left the meeting, and the church.

Over the next seven years under Fred's leadership the church grew from an average of fifty in attendance at morning worship to over one hundred. In their rather isolated community this was not insignificant. The church became entirely charismatic in its worship style. A few of the dissenting "old-timers" in the church, called "traditionalists" by most of the congregation, left the church early in Fred's tenure as pastor, but most stayed in the church.

As time went on, the traditionalists felt less and less a part of the church as new people came into the church and were placed in leadership. The new people tended to be young adults who were charismatic in their theology and experience. Worship services usually had a healing service as part of the format, and speaking in tongues was not infrequent.

A great deal of the service, which lasted anywhere from one to three hours, was devoted to group prayer, with requests being stated from the pews and many people participating in audible prayer. Choruses replaced traditional hymns. Although the hymnals remained in the pew racks, the people sang from chorus books and choruses projected on the wall with an overhead projector. People raised hands and sang sometimes loudly but always joyously.

Guitars and music synthesizers replaced the organ. The music equipment, including large loudspeakers, took up a large portion of the platform, leaving barely enough room for the pulpit and three chairs. The organ, a small pipe organ with tracker action that dated back to the late 1800s, had been kept in good repair. Organists in the area who belonged to the American Guild of Organists occasionally used it for concerts because of its historic significance and beautiful sound.

At one point during Fred's tenure, the elders considered selling the organ since it was not being used in worship. The traditionalists prevailed, however, and the organ was not sold—largely because of its historic value to the church, not because people thought it might be used again.

Tension and controversy, both of which were under the surface from the beginning of Fred's ministry, began to spill into the open. The traditionalists and charismatics disagreed over worship style and Fred's leadership style. Things came to a boiling point, and Fred announced he was leaving. He invited people to come with him to form a new church that would be charismatic in ministry and worship. Forty of the 120 attending left with Fred.

Less than a year after the split, the pastoral search committee at Community Church came to Charles and asked him to be the candidate for their pastor. The committee listed five significant issues for him to be aware of:

1. Pastoral leadership style
2. Charismatic worship style
3. Order in worship
4. Balance in lay leadership
5. Use of guitars and music synthesizers in worship versus the organ

The search committee was composed of five people, three who identified themselves as charismatic and two who said they were traditionalists. The congregation had elected them to the committee to provide a balance that would accurately reflect the church composition after the split. Although committee members had their differences, they maintained mutual respect and worked well together. Their primary concern was to find a pastor who could minister to both groups and hold the church together. Many remembered Charles as a seminary student working there prior to the team ministry with Bruce and Fred, and they appreciated his ministry. So they contacted him.

When the committee presented the five significant issues to Charles, they described what they were looking for in a pastor. Regarding pastoral leadership style, they wanted someone they could work with and who would respect their gifts and abilities. Fred had been a capable leader and knew how to get things done, but he was strong-minded and tended to act without consulting lay leaders. So the church wanted a minister who would (1) be a pastor to the whole congregation; (2) be a person who would respect the gifts and abilities of the lay people; and (3) be a bridge-builder between the charismatics and the traditionalists. Leadership style was the primary issue.

The second issue was worship style. Although charismatics still outnumbered traditionalists after the split, many people in both groups wanted a worship service where everyone would be comfortable. "Can't we worship together and be happy?" many frequently asked. They were committed to be a place where diverse worship preferences could be met. They were looking for a pastor who could bring them together.

The third issue, order in worship, had more to do with overall structure of the service than what part of the service came before another part. Under Fred's leadership, services followed no plan, but things would flow along as people said they felt led of the Spirit. While some enjoyed this free-flowing style, others were uncomfortable with it. The latter group wondered aloud why the Holy Spirit could not lead in planning a structured service.

Some also thought the prayer requests, which consumed a large block of time in the service, bordered on gossip, sometimes containing information about people outside the church who did not know they were being talked about by name in prayer. Others felt the same people dominated the prayer time with their problems and needs, so that little time was given to prayers of adoration and worship expressed towards God.

Many people, including charismatics, expressed concern about speaking in tongues, which occasionally occurred in worship. When interpretation was called for, usually by someone in the congregation who had in view the teaching in 1 Corinthians 14:13–28, often there was no interpretation given. That Fred and the elders allowed this to continue without intervention frustrated people. Thus the search committee said they wanted a pastor who would not "quench the Spirit" but would also follow biblical guidelines regarding glossolalia.

The fourth issue had to do with the pastor allowing lay people an active voice in the church. This was a reaction to Fred's perceived disregard of lay people's gifts and abilities. Although people knew that most of those who liked Fred's controlling style had left the church with him, they still wanted to make sure the new pastor would work with them. One person summed up the feelings of many when she said,

"It was my church before the pastor came, and it'll still be my church after the pastor is gone." She wanted a pastor who would give himself to the task of leadership in a way that would help her develop as a Christian and build her up so that she would be stronger after the pastor left.

The last issue, the use of guitars and synthesizers rather than the organ, was a sticky one. Not everyone agreed on this, and naturally there were a few people with definite and entrenched positions on both sides. Most people wanted a balance of the two. The search committee wanted to find someone who could help them resolve this issue.

After the search committee talked with Charles about these issues, they felt he was the man for the job. He received a unanimous call to be the pastor and came to Community Church almost one year after Fred left. During that interim period, the lay people of the church led worship, usually preached, and oversaw programs.

Charles described himself as essentially Reformed in his theology. He held to a high view of the sovereignty of God as Creator, Redeemer, and Lord; the sinfulness and fallen nature of all mankind; the work of grace through Christ's substitutionary death on the cross for all who believe in Christ in order to be saved; and the guarantee of eternal salvation for all who truly believe in the gospel of Christ. It was his conviction that holding and preaching these beliefs would result in a stable church ministry.

Just before Charles became pastor of the church, he told a friend, "I believe if I faithfully preach and teach the Word of God, the church will be okay." Not that he thought there would never be problems in the church, but for him preaching and teaching God's Word was foundational to everything the church stood for and would be the basis on which the congregation would worship God, find unity in the faith, and reach out to people in need.

Charles was open to elements of charismatic worship style and theological emphasis. For some time he had felt that those like him who held to Reformed theology were not as open to the work of the Holy Spirit as they should be. So he eagerly accepted the challenge with the conviction that God would bring healing, unify the church, and use it for his glory. During the interim period before Charles's coming, the leaders had structured a worship service that lasted about an hour and a half. The service included a mixture of traditional forms of worship and charismatic elements. At the beginning and the ending of the service, the service reflected Reformed tradition, including a call to worship, invocation, singing of traditional hymns from the hymnbook to the accompaniment of the organ, responsive reading from the biblical passages included in the back of the hymnal, "pastoral prayer" (done by the lay leader), singing of the "doxology" and "gloria patri," taking of the offering, and preaching of the Word.

In the middle of the service was a half hour labeled "praise time" in the bulletin. This was a time of praise in the charismatic tradition, with free-flowing choruses accompanied by guitar and synthesizer. The singing included joyful and energetic songs along with quiet and reflective ones. Group prayer was also part of this praise time. While most people were satisfied with this, a few of the traditionalists would sit quietly and not participate in the charismatic worship portion of the service. For their part, all the charismatics participated fully in all aspects of the service.

This was the situation Charles faced when he became pastor of Community Church. Worship attendance averaged around eighty. It was clear to him that the worship service was working to the satisfaction of most people in the church and that the hurt felt by most people over the previous years of controversy and the ensuing split went deep into the fabric of people's lives. Charles threw himself into the work. People were grateful to him and Grace for their efforts to bring healing to the church and to minister to the needs of everyone. The comment of one person—that "Charles and Grace were friends of everyone"—echoed the feelings of the congregation in general.

After Charles had been at the church about a year, the charismatics and traditionalists alike began to express some dissatisfaction over the way the worship service was structured. Although people had wanted to make everyone comfortable with the worship style, the transition from traditional liturgy to a free-flowing charismatic praise service and then back to a traditional format was too abrupt, people said. Charles had been thinking the same thing and suggested they put the praise service at the beginning of the worship period, to be followed by a more traditional format.

The people liked this idea, and the plan was implemented after communicating the upcoming change to the congregation over several weeks. The plan called for lay people to lead the praise service, with Charles seated on the front pew. His presence said to the traditionalists that everything was under control. Some of them still expressed the fear of things "getting out of hand." And the charismatics saw that their desires for certain elements in worship would be respected.

To the surprise of many people, most of the traditionalists came to the praise service, though they usually did not participate in the chorus singing or give prayer requests. They participated in their own way out of a sense of solidarity with the charismatics. As one member said, "This is our church, and we'll do this together."

This plan went well. The church prospered in other ways as well. Attendance increased from an average of 80 when Charles came, to 100 when the structure of the service changed, to 150 two years later. They had to set up extra chairs in the aisles and at the back of the sanctuary to accommodate everyone.

Because of the crowd of people, the leaders talked about going to two services. They had read that going to multiple services can increase attendance. After praying, talking, and planning, they agreed to begin two morning worship services. And since the church was moving to two services, why not make one more traditional and the other more charismatic in structure? It sounded like a good idea.

They implemented the plan and everyone in the church supported it. Attendance grew from 150 to 170 within two months. With the onset of summer, however, they planned to return to one morning service for the summer and to evaluate whether to continue two services in the fall. Many saw the change in schedule for the summer as necessary to accommodate the number of church people who worked in the tourist trade and were often unable to attend worship on Sunday morning.

The charismatic church members, however, wanted to continue with the worship service they preferred, so the leaders developed a plan for the summer in which the morning service would be in the tradition of Reformed worship and an evening service would be established in the tradition of charismatic worship. (The church did not previously have a regular evening service.) This schedule also fit the Sunday employment schedule of many of the church members.

When the new summer schedule began, to everyone's surprise the attendance at the evening service was only around twenty-five, not the seventy-five to one hundred expected. Whether this was due to people not being accustomed to an evening service or conflict with work schedules was not clear. It was also possible that Charles's decision not to attend the evening service was a factor.

Charles had based his decision on his growing perception that some of the charismatic people thought his presence at the service was having a "dampening effect" on their expressions, as they put it. So Charles thought his not attending would allow people more freedom to express themselves in worship.

Soon after the evening service began, however, Charles began to hear comments that people who attended the evening meeting were talking about forming a new church in the charismatic tradition. Charles and the elders met with the leaders of the evening worship service for frank and open discussion on the issues.

The charismatic leaders said they thought that if they formed their own church, they would grow in numbers and not be hindered by people who preferred a traditional form of worship. This surprised Charles and the elders since they thought both groups were coexisting with respect and a modicum of appreciation for each other. When the leaders asked what had changed, the charismatic group didn't respond.

The discussion, however, brought agreement that the charismatic group would remain in the church and attempts at facilitating worship that would meet diverse preferences would continue. There was general relief in the congregation at this decision since many members said they did not want to go through another church split. A handful of the charismatics did decide to leave the church.

With feelings of disappointment over the fact that a few people left the church, when the summer drew to a close the congregation and the leaders evaluated whether to return to two distinct morning services. The decision was to return to a single morning service after Labor Day. The service would follow the previous pattern of having a thirty-minute praise service that was followed by a one-hour service in the Reformed tradition.

Things went well at the church after this, although attendance gradually decreased to an average of ninety in two years. During this time, discussion continued over the format of the worship service and the style of music. Finally Charles and the elders decided to do a formal survey of the church to ascertain the desires of the people and settle the issue once and for all.

The questionnaire listed a variety of elements in the worship service, including type of songs, number of songs, type of accompaniment, time spent in prayer, structure of the prayer time, type and length of the sermon, Bible reading, kinds of congregational responses, lay or pastoral leading of worship, the use of testimonies, speaking in tongues, giving words of prophecy, and services of healing. The leaders hoped the responses would show a definite pattern towards one style or the other. Many people had begun to say they could go one way or the other, but they preferred the church would make a decision for one format and not try to do both.

Respondents were to check whether the item was important or unimportant to them, and whether they liked or disliked the particular element. A five-point scale was used to reflect nuances of opinion and feeling. The church mailed the questionnaire to approximately 150 church members and adherents. Ninety-six people responded, which was a fairly high 64 percent return, so the results were viewed as reliable.

The survey indicated that the church was almost evenly divided on what was thought important or unimportant in worship, and what individuals liked or disliked. Charles and the elders realized that two separate congregations were worshiping side by side. The question was, could this be sustained, or was there a better way to organize themselves for the glory of God and the good of his people? Had the goodwill of the people wanting to keep the church together run its course? Had it been a real expression of unity that brought people together for several years combining worship and music styles in one service, or had it only been a show of unity?

These were the questions going through Charles's mind as he reflected on the survey results. The potential for discord on the matter was high, and Charles did not want to preside over a church split. However, he knew that doing nothing was not an option.

Charles reached for his recorder and began to dictate the options he saw. In his mind was not only the question *Can we worship together and be happy?* but *Should* we worship together and be happy? Tomorrow's elders meeting was a significant time in the history of the church, and the elders were looking to him for guidance. What should he recommend?

11

What Would Lonnie Say to George?

Money/Leadership

*L*onnie looked at his appointment calendar. George was finally coming in to see him today—the visit had been much on Lonnie's mind.

As pastor of First Baptist Church, Lonnie was thrilled when George approached him and said he wanted to talk about whether God was calling him into the ministry, and consequently to seminary for study. What pastor would not be excited when a member of the church felt called to ministry, since the pastor's ministry may have contributed to the call? But Lonnie also knew it would not be easy for George and his family, just as it had not been easy for him and his family.

George was in his thirties, and although he was not in debt, he did not have much money in savings. With a depressed housing market, there wasn't much hope of selling his house at a price high enough to give George the necessary funds to go to seminary without working. With a wife and two young children, George would have to work hard to make ends meet, and both he and his wife wanted her to stay home with the children. Knowing that Lonnie and his family had faced a similar challenge, George had asked for an appointment.

Lonnie wondered if he should tell George just how hard it had been—and still was, for that matter. But they had made it, even though the process had left some scars. On the other hand, the financial struggle had taught him something about the faithfulness and timing of God.

As he collected his thoughts in preparation for seeing George, Lonnie's mind began retracing the steps leading to his own Christian conversion and call to ministry. Now at age forty-eight he was in his third year as pastor of First Baptist Church, his first church since graduating from seminary. Changing vocational direction in midlife had not been easy, but difficulties were nothing new.

Lonnie had become a Christian thirteen years ago when he and Bev were separated. Bev had become a Christian first, after seeing a psychologist about their marital distress. The county mental health agency had referred her to this psychologist—who turned out to be a Christian. Bev had grown up as the daughter of an Episcopal rector but had never really embraced Christian faith and teaching as her own. She was also shy by nature and easily intimidated. Lonnie, on the other hand, was outgoing and self-confident. They met in college and were married shortly after their graduation.

For several years prior to their separation, Lonnie and Bev had been drifting apart. Lonnie had pursued his career in the fast lane. His efforts in the marketing field had paid off. He had established his own business, which though small was quite successful. But success in that business meant he was seldom home. Neither his two young daughters nor Bev saw much of him in those days. To make matters worse, Lonnie was involved in semiprofessional sports and also the local drama group. Both he and Bev were unhappy and were searching for something to make life better.

Lonnie moved out of the house to escape the awkwardness and discomfort he felt with Bev when he was home. They had little in common and could scarcely carry on a conversation. But his relief in separating from Bev was short-lived. Bev decided, quite uncharacteristically, to get help for herself and the marriage, taking the initiative in finding a marriage counselor. What's more, she *insisted* that Lonnie get counseling too.

So Lonnie began to see the same psychologist Bev was seeing, but in separate sessions. The counselor's wisdom and care, insight and helpfulness had an impact upon Lonnie, and six months later he, too, committed his life to Christ. He and Bev were nurtured in their newfound faith by a Christian couple referred to them by the psychologist. By this time Lonnie and Bev were back together and were working to make their marriage strong.

Lonnie and Bev soon found a church that was essentially an independent church maintaining loose affiliation with other churches of like mind and practice in the area. It was everything they were looking for, and it became their church home. The liveliness of the people and worship services, the teaching, and the church's concern to meet spiritual needs in the world provided the opportunity for Lonnie and Bev to grow in their faith and develop their gifts for ministry.

As Lonnie and Bev became more active in the church, they developed a close relationship with the pastor and his wife and two other couples in the church. These four couples would pray and study and talk together for hours. They began to feel a common concern for establishing a church in another part of the country. In due course they determined that God was leading them to act in faith in this endeavor, so they all pulled up stakes and moved across the country to begin the new church-planting venture.

The plan was for the three couples to obtain employment in the area to support themselves but also to work as coleaders in establishing the church. The three couples would support the pastor financially so he would be free to give his full attention to the church.

Back when these four couples had been praying and talking together about the new church venture, Lonnie began to sense God's calling him into the ministry of teaching, preaching, and pastoring on a full-time basis as a pastor and not a layman. The more he had engaged in lay ministry, the more he felt the need for biblical and theological education. When the four families relocated to start the new church, Lonnie had his wife's full support and the blessing of the other couples to attend a seminary in the area.

Thus at age forty, Lonnie with his wife Bev, age thirty-eight, and their two teenage daughters, ages sixteen and thirteen, put their house up for sale, sold the business, and moved across the country. It was a big step to make such a move, but they were in it together and were convinced God was leading them and would meet their needs.

They planned to sell the house and use the proceeds to finance their educational and living expenses until Lonnie graduated from seminary. When they put the house up for sale, however, the local economy was in recession, and the housing market was depressed. The house had not sold when they moved, so they made arrangements for some friends to rent the house until it sold. Lonnie sold his business for three thousand dollars, and it was this money in hand that started Lonnie and Bev on their new venture of faith.

Financial problems developed almost immediately. The first semester at school went well for Lonnie. The money from selling the business had enabled him to devote his full time and energy to his studies. He had been unsure of his academic abilities after being out of school so long, but he quickly regained his academic skills. He was confident he could get a part-time job for the second semester and continue his studies with no difficulty, and he assumed their house would sell any day.

But the house did not sell. To make matters worse, the friends renting the house left abruptly in January, and the rent income left with them. The mortgage, however, still needed to be paid monthly, so Lonnie had to scramble to work something out with the bank to cover it.

When the renters vacated the house, they neglected to shut off the water or electricity. During an unusual cold spell, the pipes froze and burst, causing extensive damage throughout the house. Had it not been for a neighbor who noticed water running down the driveway, the damage might have been worse. Insurance paid for much of the repairs, but the house sat empty for several months during repairs.

Six months after the first renters left, their real estate agent found new renters. Those renters stayed for only a short time and then left. Again the bills piled up while the house was vacant. The agent located new renters. These new people trashed the house as badly as the water had damaged it before. The result was more vacancy and more bills. Lonnie lowered the price of the house, and still it did not sell.

Because of the long distance involved, Lonnie felt he had no control over the situation. He could not afford to fly back to the area to arrange matters himself. His only options were to trust the real estate agent to do his best and to commit the whole situation to God. Lonnie tried to put it out of his mind, but the unsold house was a continual burden.

When Lonnie began seminary, he and Bev found a house to rent and were able to arrange for an option to buy the house within one year. Finding a house to rent in their price range near the seminary had been no small feat. Housing costs were high. Lonnie and Bev had made a quick trip to the area a few months before moving there to arrange for their housing, and it was not until late the night before they were to fly back home that they finalized the deal on a small house barely adequate for a family of four.

After Lonnie had been at seminary for a year, the first house still had not sold, and the date for exercising the option to buy the house they were renting was fast approaching. Lonnie had secured a part-time job in public relations work and received a generous scholarship from the seminary during the second semester of his first year. Bev, too, had found work teaching at a Christian school, but the salary was quite low. With frugal living, however, they managed to get by, though several back bills remained unpaid.

Two weeks before the final day for exercising the option to buy the house they were renting—or it would be put up for sale—some friends "out of the blue" offered to supply the down payment on the house in exchange for 50 percent co-ownership in the house. Lonnie and Bev would pay their share of the down payment by making the full monthly mortgage payment on their own. They could do this for slightly more than the monthly rent they were already paying and could begin to build up some equity in the house. Thus again at "the eleventh hour" they were able to arrange for housing in spite of their first house not selling. Lonnie saw God's timing as "a bit scary, but nevertheless faithful."

Lonnie had not registered for his second year at seminary when classes ended his first year, mostly as a test of whether the Lord had indeed called him to seminary. The financial struggle was a constant worry. And in the church planting venture, Lonnie and the other core couples had gone separate ways after several strong disagreements with the pastor. This had shaken Lonnie deeply since his primary motivation for moving had been the church planting ministry.

It was the financial struggle, however, that was the most wearying for Lonnie and the family. They economized in every way possible, eating little and buying only essentials. But they still fell further behind in paying bills. In one particularly embarrassing incident a creditor repossessed the car Lonnie was leasing literally in the dark of night. He was only one month behind in lease payments and felt embarrassed and angry when the car was repossessed. *This is what happens to losers and deadbeats, not respectable people,* he thought. Now his family was left with an old clunker of a car in need of extensive costly repairs they could not afford. But it ran, and they prayed and prayed it would keep running. Meanwhile creditors were dunning them with letters and phone calls demanding payment. So Lonnie prepared to get a full-time job to catch up on expenses. Seminary would have to be postponed, Lonnie reasoned. The thought discouraged him, but he saw no other option. The day before classes began—Lonnie still had not registered to begin his second year—the seminary called to inform him that the school had just received a scholarship to be used by someone who had left a business career to come to seminary. "Would you be interested in receiving this scholarship?" the financial aid officer asked. Lonnie just about cried.

The scholarship amounted to full tuition. God's timing was again to provide at the last minute. With school expenses covered, the income from his part-time job and Bev's job would have to take care of the rest of their expenses, though he knew their incomes were still not sufficient to make ends meet. *If only the house would sell!* he thought.

When Christmas approached that second year at seminary, the family agreed not to exchange gifts; rather, they would give one another messages of love and affection. But a few days before Christmas Lonnie received a cash gift in his mailbox from an anonymous donor, enabling them to have a small celebration in addition to the verbal messages of love. *Last minute again,* he thought.

Financial problems were not the only stress on Lonnie. Lonnie's sister and her two teenage sons had to move in with his family. His sister had recently been divorced and was facing a debilitating disease. She had lost her house and financial security through the divorce, and the medical disability payments she received did not come close to meeting her expenses. So for five months seven people lived in a house barely adequate for four. Compounding the stress was the anger and misbehavior of the boys who were having difficulty adjusting to life without their father.

Lonnie and Bev felt quite sure that God had led them to come to seminary. They saw themselves as responsible people who were more than willing to make sacrifices to serve the Lord, but often they were tired and confused about their living and financial situation. At times they were embarrassed and humiliated to be in such desperate circumstances.

Somehow in spite of their struggles Lonnie was able to finish his M.Div. program in four years. He and the family decided to stay in the area another year after he finished so his youngest daughter could finish her final year of high school. With Lonnie and Bev both working full-time, they now made some headway paying back bills, but the house across the country still had not sold. Meanwhile Lonnie had put the house they presently lived in up for sale shortly after graduating from seminary, and it had not sold either. *Wonderful!* he thought. *Now I own two houses, can't pay for them, and can't sell them!* To make matters worse, a church had invited him to candidate, and the church did not own a parsonage. "This gives new meaning to the phrase 'house poor,'" he joked with a friend.

But God had been faithful in the past, and Lonnie knew he could trust God for the future. At least most of the time he thought that way. There were times when he worried about finances. "The financial area of my life is the hardest for me to give to the Lord," he confided to a friend. But had not God come through before when no solution was in sight? This encouraged him to keep on trusting God and committing the selling of the houses to him.

Candidating at First Baptist Church was itself something of a miracle. Lonnie had known of the church, which was a three hour drive from his seminary, and he felt his gifts and desires for ministry matched the church's needs and mission. But while Lonnie was unaffiliated with any denomination, First Baptist Church was committed to its denomination and was receiving home missions support from that group. A denominational leader was serving as the interim pastor and had flatly refused for Lonnie's name to come to the search committee. Someone else had suggested Lonnie for supply preaching when the denominational official was away. Lonnie did preach that Sunday, and the contact eventually led to his receiving a call to be their pastor.

So at age forty-five, five years after pulling up stakes, giving up his career in the marketing field, moving with his family across country to seminary, and still owning two houses he could not afford, he became the pastor of First Baptist Church. Trusting God for finances, however, was not over—nor was God's provision.

Finding adequate housing was the immediate problem for Lonnie and Bev. They had rented their home at seminary to one of their daughters and two of her friends, so that the mortgage would be covered until the house sold. But Lonnie could not buy another house without getting the assets out of at least one of his two houses, nor could he afford the high rents in the area of First Baptist Church. Again Lonnie and Bev got on their knees to pray and seek direction from God.

A family in the church had to be away on business for a period of time and offered Lonnie their house while they were away. Then two weeks after arriving at First Baptist Church, their first house finally sold—and for the original asking price. It had taken five years, but the house sold just in time to provide the down payment on a house near First Baptist Church. Once again at the last minute God had provided for their needs.

One year later, the house near the seminary also sold. They divided the assets with the friends who had made the initial down payment, which left a little money to catch up on some back bills. But finances were still tight. Half his salary from First Baptist Church went to pay the mortgage on their present house, a much higher percentage than the one-third recommended by financial experts, but Lonnie saw no other way. He and Bev rarely bought new clothes and certainly didn't eat too much. Cutting down on food consumption was one way of saving money, but friends sometimes commented that Lonnie and Bev were too thin. Lonnie also worried about his poor credit rating and felt badly that his Christian testimony may have been weakened by his financial problems.

Looking back on the last five years as he prepared to meet with George, who was considering a similar path, Lonnie could see God's faithfulness. He saw it all along the way as well, and was grateful and humbled by how God had supplied his needs, although he often wished God's timing had been different. He had not known when he started down this road that finances would be such a problem. Had he been obedient to God? Should he have done things differently? Did he make some mistakes? How would God use this for his glory? Would people be offended if they knew Lonnie's financial situation?

Lonnie knew his own experience had served to deepen his life of prayer and desire to walk obediently with God, but he disliked the times of worry and last minute arrangements. He was weary. At age forty-eight he still had twenty or so years of pastoral ministry ahead of him as the Lord might allow, and he hoped those years would not be like the past eight. His immediate concern was what to say to George. He prayed for guidance. "What should I say to George?" he whispered.

12

Who Needs to Forgive Whom?

Forgiveness/Leadership

*B*ob felt a strange mixture of anger and peace within. In recent weeks he had been aware of his emotions in a new way. And the insights he had gained into how his family background had contributed to who he now was had a liberating effect on him, causing him to feel more secure than he ever felt before. At the same time he was aware that the anger that had been diffused in the past was now boiling to the surface, and he wondered how to handle it. So many changes were happening inside of him so fast. At age fifty-seven he looked back on his life with pain and regret. His past haunted him, but he wanted the future to be different.

Bob had gone to seminary at age forty-five after a successful career of nearly twenty years in a secular organization that specialized in fitness and health activities. In this company he concentrated on working with health clubs that were experiencing difficulties, and he was instrumental in helping club after club to turn around. He had the ability to infuse new vision and develop quality programs in dying clubs. How ironic that he could help those clubs become strong at the very time he suffered inner agony and turmoil himself. Bob had not gotten over his dysfunctional family background.

Bob's father, Hans, was a well-known Lutheran minister. Hans was a charming and energetic pastor who was active and respected throughout the denomination. Bob liked his father but rarely saw him. Bob's mother, Trudy, made up for his father's lack of attention by smothering Bob with attention, both as a child and as an adult. She saw Bob as her "miracle baby." Trudy had only one ovary, and her doctor said it was unlikely she would ever conceive. But she did become pregnant and gave birth to twins at that!

As children, both Bob and his twin sister had many allergies, but only his sister was treated medically for them. Bob's mother saw him as "just a nervous child," and she poured out more love on him to make him better. At the same time, Hans was distant and formal with Bob, due perhaps to his German background. Bob just knew that his sister got their father's attention, and he got their mother's.

Looking back on his childhood, Bob realized his mother and father had a strange relationship. They never seemed close and argued incessantly, but they never mentioned divorce. Both Hans and Trudy were strong-willed Germans. Hans's father was an alcoholic, but alcohol abuse had never been a problem for Hans himself. Trudy's mother had shown partiality, shunning Trudy in favor of Trudy's sister. Bob now realized his parents were products of their past. Hans was like his father in being distant and formal in family relationships but outgoing and warm in public. Trudy imitated her mother by showing favoritism toward one child.

Bob's mother once told him that when she and Hans returned from their honeymoon, "Hans was a basket case." She indicated that Hans had difficulty being intimate either emotionally or sexually with her. Bob could never recall his parents being affectionate in front of him.

Bob's father did teach him how to throw and hit a ball, and Bob played organized baseball, but he could never recall his father coming to see him play. Bob played other sports in junior high and high school, and his father would buy him various kinds of athletic equipment, but again he wouldn't come to see him compete.

In high school Bob began to find his identity in sports. He was good in sports and was readily accepted by others for his athletic activities. This made him feel masculine when little else did. Such affirmation helped set the direction of his studying sports and fitness activities in college and graduate school. Even as he pursued the "manly" area of athletics, however, his mother still treated him as a little boy. Until the time of her death when he was forty, she still called him junior. And he blushed every time he recalled an incident on the day he received his M.S.—his mother came to him after the graduation ceremony and said in the presence of many other people, "How's my little apple blossom today?" Even when he was an adult, at restaurants his mother would try to order his meal from the menu. *Is it something in me or in her that caused her to be so controlling?* he wondered on many occasions. But he never did anything about it since he didn't know what to do.

Perhaps his submission to people he viewed as authorities went back to his early childhood. He remembered an incident when he was three in which he broke twenty-three windowpanes in the house after his parents made him stay inside. His parents told relatives they "had to beat the aggression out of Bob." So on the one hand they punished Bob and restricted his activities, but on the other hand his mother smothered him with affection and "lovey-dovey" talk. Relatives wondered how Bob and his twin sister would turn out because of the strange relationship Hans and Trudy had with each other and the way they treated the children. Several people spoke of the unhealthy bond Trudy had with Bob.

Bob knew from his studies that his background could have affected his sexual identity. For some people, a distant father and a smothering mother contributed to their sexual orientation as homosexuals. But it did not appear to have this effect on him. He was thoroughly heterosexual. As Bob reflected in recent months on all these experiences, he was aware of intense anger within him, an anger that could be explosive, he knew, but seemed more like what Henri Nouwen calls "frozen anger," the kind of anger that is deeply entrenched but just sits there numbing the person. He realized his aggressiveness in sports and his high-energy attacking of organizational problems were displacements for the anger, but the numbness would not go away no matter how hard he worked or how much he understood.

Colleagues and friends weren't aware of his anger because Bob covered it up by doing the right thing, being outgoing and friendly, and taking on big responsibilities. His anger was private. His wife, Leslie, and their four children knew about it, however, for occasionally he would explode in a verbal tirade; but for the most part he turned his anger in on himself.

Bob's anger expressed itself in several ways. He had an extraordinarily high need to please and be accepted by people, so he worked to be successful and would not do anything that might make others upset with him. He also had become hypercritical of himself; he didn't regard what he did as worthwhile. The harder he worked to please others and be accepted by them, the more he felt like a failure. He was in a bottomless pit.

One of Bob's biggest difficulties was handling criticism from others. Criticism caused him to crumble. On the outside he would smile and receive the criticism without comment, but on the inside he was dying. His response was either to make excuses to himself or to feel utterly worthless. He never fought back, tried to clarify what was said, defended himself, or saw his failure as an honest mistake to learn from. Churning with anger, he either felt "I am inadequate" or "You are a louse for doing this to me." But he kept on smiling.

All his life, Bob had been a slave to others' expectations. Even his decision to go to seminary was in part due to the influence of others. While he was still in the health and fitness field, he became a lay preacher in his denomination. Preaching and ministering to people brought him much satisfaction because people gave him compliments. Many people suggested he consider going to seminary and being a full-time pastor like his father. When he was thirty-five he began to wrestle with a call to ministry and spent six intense weeks in inner debate, but finally decided not to pursue full-time ministry yet.

Five years later, however, as others continued to encourage him to consider seminary, he obtained an application from his denominational school, where his father had been well-known. As he filled out the application, he came to a question asking for comments about his personal commitment to ministry. He couldn't write anything, knowing the influence of others on him and not his own commitment had taken him to this point. He so much wanted to please others that he had been willing to change careers if others thought it was a good idea. He decided once again not to pursue seminary studies yet.

In the next few years a series of events changed Bob's mind. First he and Leslie attended a camp retreat held by evangelical Christians. The enthusiasm, commitment, and joy exhibited by others were new experiences for Bob and Leslie. They attended more meetings of this group and gradually came to the conclusion that they should leave the denomination of their parents and their own lifelong affiliation and join an evangelical church. It was a difficult choice. Bob said, "It feels like I'm walking out on my father."

Bob began working as a counselor to young people experiencing difficulties with drug and alcohol addiction, and he developed a friendship with another man in the ministry who was a mature Christian. Bob was becoming extremely dissatisfied with his health and fitness company due to their changing program emphasis, chronic budget problems, and high staff turnover, and when he shared that with his friend in the ministry, his friend encouraged him to consider seminary. Bob brought it up to Leslie, and she, knowing his longtime interest in the ministry, also strongly encouraged him to go to seminary. Her comment "turned on a light" for him, and he made application to a seminary, a different school than he started to apply to five years ago. On this application there was no question about personal commitment to ministry, but Bob could have answered it in the affirmative. In his soul, his commitment to ministry was one he could now own for himself.

Going to seminary at age forty-five was no small task for Bob and his family. He had four teenage children to care for, and Bob soon felt overwhelmed with his studies. He looked at the other students, most of whom were younger than he was, and thought they were perfect. Money was tight, even though Bob continued to work long and hard in the health and fitness field to earn a living. It took Bob five years to complete seminary.

After Bob completed seminary, he couldn't find an opening in a church. Again he felt angry—at himself for being so inadequate that no church wanted him, at God for leading him to seminary where he had worked so hard only to be unemployable in the church at age fifty, and at the ministry itself, which took his father from him and was so demanding of all who gave themselves to it.

In September after his graduation from seminary, he spoke at a retreat that a friend had arranged for him to attend. When he finished speaking, a person came up to him and asked if he would consider being pastor of the church where this man attended and chaired the pastoral search committee. Bob inquired about the details and learned it was a church where he had sent his dossier earlier and had been rejected as a potential candidate. He did, however, become a candidate at this church and was promptly called to be the pastor.

He had now been pastor of this church for seven years. When he came, the church had many problems: low attendance, mostly older people in the congregation, low budget, no vision or outreach. In many ways the situation resembled the health clubs where he worked for many years. Once again, his drive and need to please people kicked into action.

Over these seven years the church had stabilized, the budget became strong, they had begun new programs, and he was faithfully proclaiming the redemptive work of God in Christ; but Bob was still uneasy. Did people really like him? The slightest criticism—real or imagined—still devastated him. He was beginning to think he should move to a new ministry.

Looking back, Bob realized that while in seminary he had harbored anger towards God. The studies were hard, money was in short supply, and he saw little of Leslie and the children. It was all very wearying. He wasn't even sure now whether he had been a Christian when he began seminary. He did make a definite commitment to Christ at the end of his first year in seminary through the influence of a friend. Perhaps his struggles about entering seminary and his uncertainty about vocation and denomination were all reflections of his anger towards his father and God. They were both rather distant, and he wanted them to be close; but he couldn't do anything about it.

To make matters worse, it now dawned on Bob that to a large extent he had repeated the pattern of his father's relationship with him in his relationships with his own children. He had difficulty being close to his children. As they

153

got older he felt inadequate and incapable of guiding them or even being with them. Was this how his father felt with him? Regarding his marriage, Bob felt it was a miracle that he and Leslie had made it this far. The first ten years of their marriage had gone well, but then Leslie began to be critical of him, causing Bob to withdraw into silence and avoid relating to her or the children. When they got married, she needed someone to care for and he needed someone to mother him, so she did the mothering and he the enjoying. But as time passed she tired of that role. Leslie's respect for him waned, and she grew critical. The more critical she was, the more he became critical of himself, creating in Bob an utter sense of worthlessness and despair. He had no sense of identity and was groping to find his way in life, as reflected in his desire for others to tell him what to do. Dependency on others increased his anger towards himself and others. It was a vicious circle.

In public Bob and Leslie gave the appearance of having a healthy marriage. When they went to marriage retreats, they gave all the right answers and were seen by others as a model couple.

But then their marriage gradually began to improve. He and Leslie began to work hard to improve their communication. Their expectations changed, and they matured. When the children left home to be on their own, Bob and Leslie's relationship settled into a comfortable routine of mutual acceptance and appreciation. Bob saw the grace of God at work in it all.

As Bob reflected on all these things, his mind returned to the significant breakthrough that occurred just six weeks ago. He had attended a prayer retreat, and as he spent much time alone in prayer, he felt an unusual presence of the Lord giving him insight into his inner fears and anger. With new clarity he saw the issues he needed to deal with to be a whole person with God and people. He listed the issues:

- An excessive need for approval
- An unhealthy bonding to his mother (sometimes referring to her in the present tense even though she had died seventeen years before)
- A love-hate relationship with his father (also referring to him occasionally in the present tense even though he had died thirty-six years before)
- Anger towards God
- Poor self-image

He shared these insights with a pastor friend who affirmed and encouraged him. God used this person's acceptance toward Bob as a healing balm. He had spoken to someone about his pain and background and was not condemned for it. In addition Bob had been reading about dysfunctional families for the past several years. God had used that reading to give him insight into his own situation.

At any rate, the last six weeks had begun a healing process within Bob. He was more accepting of himself and his anger towards himself and others, and his feelings of inadequacy were dissipating. He was even beginning to enjoy the love of God. He wondered if God was forgiving him, or if he was forgiving God. At age fifty-seven he was beginning to feel a freedom he had never felt before.

He knew things were not perfect. He was still vulnerable to the old patterns. The church had reached a plateau, and he wondered if they and he needed a change. And his relationship with Leslie, although happily being redefined, still had some awkward issues that needed to be addressed. Facing difficulties was not easy for him, but it was easier now than before. New questions were arising: Why did it take so long for healing to begin? What's going to happen in the future? How can I use what I've learned to help others?

13

What Should Sally Do?

Divorce and Remarriage

$\mathcal{S}$ally sat nervously fingering her scarf. She had come to talk with some friends about whether she should grant the divorce requested by her husband, Tom. She was a Christian and had always looked at divorce as wrong, something God did not want his children to do, something that meant failure on the part of a husband and wife. She was committed to the marriage and to working things out with Tom, but she was also troubled by mounting evidence of Tom's unfaithfulness and by rebellion in their two teenage sons. And she knew the stress of recent years was taking its toll on her.

With hesitancy and a shaky voice she began to review the last twenty years of her life. Sally met Tom at the Christian liberal arts college where both attended. Tom had been a year ahead of her. He was popular, outgoing, and always surrounded by friends. As a good-looking and athletically gifted man, he had no trouble attracting female admirers.

Late in Sally's freshman year, Tom asked her for a date. She was shocked—since he was engaged to another woman—so she refused his offer graciously but firmly. Rather than putting him off, however, her refusal challenged him, and he turned on the charm. Shortly after he first asked Sally for a date, Tom broke off his engagement to the other woman and informed Sally he was now free to date her. For a while Sally continued to deny his requests for dates, but she was finally won over by his charm, good looks, and self-confidence. She agreed to go out with him but "played it cool," since she was not sure she could trust someone who would break off his engagement to date her.

Although Sally was a very attractive woman and had dated men before going out with Tom, he was the first man she had ever kissed. She had been raised in a strong, loving, and supportive Christian home. Life had been happy and uncomplicated for her. Tom's childhood, on the other hand, had been difficult. His parents were divorced when he was eight months old, and he lived with his father, who remarried when Tom was ten years old. He did not meet his biological mother until he was nineteen. Tom's father was distant, punitive, and had a drinking problem, and Tom's stepmother was cruel to him.

When Sally and Tom began to date, she occasionally worried about his background and the effect it might have on him, but he was so self-confident and articulate she thought he must have worked it through. And other college women considered him quite a find.

When Tom graduated from college, he and Sally were married. During their first year of marriage she finished college and Tom began seminary studies to prepare for pastoral ministry, to which he had felt called for some time. Sally was thrilled, but a little scared to be married to a man going into the ministry. With both of them working part-time jobs and Tom studying hard and doing field education as a youth leader in a nearby church, they didn't see much of each other that first year of marriage. But Sally was happy and viewed their marriage as strong. She deeply loved Tom and saw his love for her as more than satisfying.

One concern Sally did have in the early days of their marriage was Tom liked to spend money when she thought they should be more frugal. His spending habits meant they did not always have enough money to pay their regular bills, and it bothered her that some things had to be paid late. Once he bought a dog without discussing it with her. She was surprised, but if that was what he wanted, she was happy to go along with it. She thought she understood him, and since she did not want to create difficulty between them, she said nothing.

After about eighteen months of marriage, one night Tom did not come home until one in the morning, and Sally did not know where he was. He told her he met someone and was witnessing to that person about the Christian faith. She believed him and was relieved that he was not hurt. This began a pattern of his staying out late without informing her of his plans. She knew many people were coming to him for counsel, and she was pleased he was using his gifts to help people, but she was often lonely and wished she knew where he was. She was especially hurt one night when they were invited out to dinner with friends. She was not feeling well from her first pregnancy, so he left her alone and went out with their friends.

After seminary, the Congregational church where Tom had done his field education called him to be their pastor. The pastor under whom Tom had worked as a youth leader had just run off with a woman in the parish, abandoning his family and destroying hers, and the church was going through a very difficult time. The people loved Tom, and with his considerable gifts, people saw him as the logical choice to be their pastor. Tom and Sally ministered in the church for six years, and during that time the church grew in numbers, programs, and outreach. Such growth was unusual in an area of Wisconsin where church growth usually came in small increments, if at all. By this time, Tom and Sally had two young sons, and Sally felt life was going great.

Then the first blow came. When Tom and Sally returned from vacation, the deacons of the church confronted Tom with the news that six women in the church had revealed to them they had had sexual affairs with Tom over the span of time he had been in the church. Tom denied it all and accused the women of being hysterical and mentally ill people whom he had helped in counseling but whose word could not be trusted. Sally had heard that this kind of thing sometimes happened to pastors, and she believed her husband without any doubts. Tom showed her a great deal of attention, writing love notes and sending her flowers regularly. Surely he would not behave that way towards her and be involved with other women, Sally reasoned.

Still, the deacons insisted that Tom leave. So the following Sunday he read his resignation from the pulpit and left through the back door without greeting anyone after the service. In his resignation announcement he admitted to no guilt or indiscretion. He told Sally he was leaving to appease the deacons and spare the church from difficulty.

Another Congregational church, also in Wisconsin, immediately called Tom to be their pastor. Church attendance and programs increased as in his first church. Tom was a gifted preacher and good organizer, and he had unusual ability in relating to people. People were drawn to him as metal to a magnet because of his charm and dynamic personality. But two years after arriving at this church, Tom suddenly resigned and left the church within a few days. Sally was stunned. She learned later why Tom had resigned so abruptly. A man had threatened to kill Tom after he learned from his wife that Tom was having an affair with her.

Although the congregation held a hastily organized but big party for Tom before he left, many people were surprised to learn that Tom had moved to an adjoining town to begin a new church not affiliated with any denomination. Tom advertised in the local paper for two weeks, and three hundred people came for worship on the first Sunday. Tom had many friends and contacts in the community, including friends from golf tournaments at the local country club where he was active, and their influence on their friends resulted in a strong church being organized very quickly. Many people became Christians, the church developed a solid discipleship program, and several young people made decisions to enter Christian ministry as a result of the church's witness and particularly because of Tom's dynamic leadership.

While Tom and Sally were serving at this third church, one day Sally opened a music book on the piano at home and discovered a letter to Tom from a young college woman in the church describing her joy over the sexual relationship she was having with Tom. Sally was shocked and felt an overwhelming sense of panic. She immediately called Tom, but as he had done before, he claimed it was not true but just another hysterical woman he had tried to help. He also said he resented being interrupted while preparing for a funeral. Sally did not know he was doing a funeral that day or any time soon. A few minutes later the young woman who wrote the letter knocked on the door and told Sally the letter was not true. "It was just an emotional attachment to Tom. I made those things up. Nothing really happened," she said. When Tom came home that night, he was upset with Sally for believing the contents of the letter and for being upset with him.

Sally felt guilty for causing such a fuss. And for the first time she recognized that was how Tom had made her feel each time there had been a question about his activities. Tom would accuse her of being too gullible, and this would make her feel guilty. She would wonder if she was doing something wrong to make Tom want to look for satisfaction with another woman, and this made her feel even more guilty. Even being suspicious of him made her feel guilty.

Sally was also afraid of Tom. When their younger son was two years old, Tom was hitting him repeatedly for something he had done, and Sally intervened to protect her son. Tom turned on her, hitting her and suffocating her, to the point that she almost lost consciousness and feared she would die. Her face was so badly bruised she did not leave the house for several days. She decided she had better not confront Tom directly about anything in the future, or she and the boys might be hurt. This fear was on her mind when she called Tom about the letter in the music book, but she felt such anxiety she could not help but call.

Finally, after being at the church for four years, their marriage began to unravel. Tom told Sally that he was no longer attracted to her and that for most of their marriage he had not loved her. He said he wanted a divorce. He asked her to pray about it and give him a little time to work out the necessary details. Sally was devastated. She felt completely betrayed and lonely. The following Sunday when Tom preached, Sally somehow found great encouragement listening to him, and she came away from the service thinking she and Tom could work out their problems. A powerful and loving God could do anything, and she trusted him to intervene in her marriage, so she told Tom she did not want a divorce.

Soon afterwards another accusation of adultery surfaced. A woman went to the leaders and stated that Tom had been conducting an affair with her for two years. She said he had initiated it, and she had only recently begun to deal with her own guilt over it. When the leaders confronted Tom, he denied the whole thing and said the woman was crazy. In the middle of the meeting with the leaders, Tom calmly excused himself to take a nap. Sally thought that his being so calm perhaps reflected his innocence. In the days that followed, several other women from the church came forward and revealed they also had been engaged in ongoing affairs with Tom for several years. Tom denied these charges as well, and Sally continued to believe him.

When the multiple accusations came, Tom, with the church leaders' backing, decided to take an overseas trip to visit missionaries who were supported by the church. The church leaders wanted time to think without Tom around since they had never experienced anything like this before and were not sure what to do.

Tom was gone for several weeks. On the day he was to return, Sally was preparing to go to the airport to meet him when she received a call from Tom saying he was already in town. The plane had arrived early, and he had gotten a ride to church.

When Tom came home that evening, Sally asked who gave him a ride from the airport—a two-hour trip. He told her not to be so suspicious, and she once again felt guilty for asking. She asked him to be more careful about ministering to women and being with women because of what people were saying. This was the first time she had been this direct with him, and the look he gave her frightened her.

The next day the church secretary hand delivered a letter to Sally from Tom. He asked for an immediate separation. Sally refused. She told Tom they should try to work things out. But Tom moved to his church office, where he had facilities to bathe and sleep. Over the next several days Sally went to the office a few times in the middle of the night but never found Tom there. She also discovered a wardrobe of clothes she assumed were Tom's but which she had never seen before.

Under continuing pressure to resign and ongoing accusations of sexual misconduct, Tom finally offered his resignation. He had plans to become pastor of a church in Arizona. At a huge farewell dinner thrown for him by the church, Tom sat at the head table with special guests while Sally and the boys ate at a far-removed table. When the master of ceremonies introduced Sally, she received a three-minute standing ovation.

He did come home that night instead of staying at the office, but he was drunk and accused Sally of dressing seductively for the dinner. Sally felt guilty about that, knowing she tried to look as attractive as she could, not to seduce men but to show everyone she was doing all right in spite of the known tension in her marriage and the accusations being leveled against her husband.

Tom left for the church in Arizona three months before the boys' school year ended, but Sally stayed with the children, now in early adolescence. The three-month period away from Tom was a lonely one for Sally and the boys. During that time Tom called them only twice, once in response to a call from the police about some minor trouble the boys were in. Sally was worried about the increasingly rebellious behavior of the boys. Their guidance counselor at school said he thought the boys were showing signs of missing their father.

For years Tom had accused her of being incompetent, but he left it to her to sell their home. Sally had doubts about her ability to handle matters, but she knew that others saw her as being much more capable than she saw herself. Shortly after the school year finished, the house did sell, and she and the boys moved to rejoin Tom.

When Sally and the boys arrived in the southwest, the first thing Tom said when he saw Sally was, "Your hair is too short. You shouldn't have done that without my permission!" Sally longed to be held by Tom, but intimacy of any sort had been absent in the relationship for a long time.

Tom continued to ask for a divorce, and Sally continued to request that they get help to work out their problems. In spite of all the allegations from women through the years, and in spite of Tom's behavior towards her and the way he lived his life, at the time she still believed his denials about having affairs with women. Even when the secretary from the third church, the one who hand delivered Tom's letter requesting a separation from Sally, moved to the Arizona church to be Tom's secretary, Sally would not let herself think much about it. She knew that executive secretaries often moved with their bosses, and Tom had indicated he could not get along without this secretary. But shortly after arriving in their new home, Sally discovered a large number of letters written to Tom by this secretary and other women describing explicit sexual details of their relationships with Tom. Reality hit Sally with full force. She could no longer deny the evidence. *He must be a pathological liar!* she admitted to herself. She sat down and dissolved in tears.

Two months after Sally had arrived in Arizona, she stood one Sunday with Tom greeting people at the end of the service. During a lull in the line, Tom leaned over and said, "I want to talk to you about a divorce, and that's final!" Before Sally could respond, more people moved in the line to greet them. Sally managed to engage in small talk with the parishioners. When they talked later that day, Tom said, "I love you with a godly love, but I am not in love with you and have not been for fifteen of our seventeen years of marriage." That day Tom forced her and the boys out of the house. Four months later, they were now staying at a motel that Tom was paying for, and they were living on one hundred dollars a week from Tom.

Sitting with her friends, Sally now asked for their advice. They said what many others had said through the years: Tom did not love her and had total disregard for the boys. Sally felt shame that Tom's mistreatment of them was so evident to others.

"Tom is a very sick man who needs help," said one of Sally's friends. "But you cannot give it to him."

"But God can do anything," replied Sally. "Tom is the first and only man I have ever loved. Besides, I believe so strongly in the permanence of marriage that I cannot think about divorce. Tom and I are both Christians. We must do the right thing. The promise I gave before God and my friends was 'for better or worse.' I took a long time to fall in love, and I can't fall out of love easily."

Sally began to cry again, not the heavy tears so frequent in the past, but quiet sobs of despair. "What is the right thing, the Christian thing to do?" she asked.

Appendix

How to Teach a Case

*T*here are as many ways to teach cases as there are individuals doing it. Thus there is no one right way, but leaders will want to accomplish the goal of involving individuals in the group with the issues in the case. Any method that accomplishes that goal is legitimate. To teach cases effectively we need to concern ourselves with three essential factors: the case itself, the teacher, and the group.

The case. Some cases portray a dominant issue but may also have several subsidiary issues. Other cases may illustrate a variety of issues without having a single dominant theme. When selecting a case for group discussion, keep in mind the main issue as well as secondary issues portrayed in the case and how these issues relate to the needs and composition of the group.

For example, you may choose a case that will get participants to talk about the dominant theme of anger in the case. Conflict management may then be a secondary theme the teacher wants to focus on. The same case can also focus primarily on conflict management, with other issues, including anger, being touched on but not given the central focus of the teaching.

When reading a case, then, jot down ideas of what the central issue of the case is and what the secondary issues are. Decide what will receive the primary attention as you develop your teaching plan. You may choose to introduce the case by identifying what you see as the central issue, and list other issues illustrated as well, or you may ask the group to identify these issues and thereby have a part in deciding what to discuss.

If you ask the group to identify issues to be discussed, it means, of course, not only that you need to have some flexibility in approaching the subject matter with your group but also some ability to lead and teach in the areas identified by the group. This may be nothing more than good skill in facilitating group discussion on your part, but it may also mean more knowledge of particular subjects than you are prepared for. Still, the approach has merit in that it allows for group participants to explore issues of interest to them. And expertise in a given area may emerge from a group participant to the benefit of the whole group.

The teacher. The role of the teacher is to facilitate group discussion around the issues of the case. In some instances, a minilecture may be appropriate. Most of the time, however, the teacher's role is to guide the discussion towards a productive end in which group members are helped to deal with the issues illustrated in the case and come to some kind of resolution of the case.

The cases in this book do not have an apparent resolution, so there can be no absolute declaration of what happened to resolve the situations. But that is part of the dynamic of case teaching. The point is not necessarily to resolve the issue to everyone's satisfaction or even to reach unanimity on what did happen or ought to happen, but rather to engage people in thinking about the issues for themselves and about what they can learn from the case to apply in their own lives.

The group. Groups also have different personalities. Some may be more reflective than others. Others may be more talkative. Some may be tentative and approach the case by probing for more information. Others may reach dogmatic conclusions quickly. The leader's task is to help the group function as a group so that both individual and group learning are maximized and not hindered by the process.

A group of experienced ministers may take a different approach discussing a particular issue than a group of seminarians. Age, denominational affiliation, and theology are also factors that will affect the mix of ideas expressed. The same case taught by the same teacher to different groups will have different outcomes. That is part of the benefit and learning potential in the case method.

We now turn to some specific suggestions for effective case teaching.

1. Know the Case Thoroughly

Read the case several times to have adequate knowledge of names and time lines as well as issues. Be aware of the content of particular pages so you can make specific reference to a point or illustration, especially of major issues you want to highlight.

Look for significant transition points in the case. Where are you surprised as you first read through the case? What does this tell you about your own involvement in the issue, and how might this affect your approach to the case? If you found something intriguing, undoubtedly others will too, so you might want to focus on this with the group.

Thorough knowledge of names, places, sequences, possible cause and effect, and specific details pertinent to the case is essential for the teacher. You should know more about the details of the case than the members of the group.

2. Have a Purpose in Mind

When preparing to teach a case, decide on the purpose you want to accomplish in the group discussion. This means you will want to identify the key issues portrayed in the case and decide how these issues relate to the needs of the group. What issues do you specifically want the group to deal with? Why?

At the end, what would you like the group to know? What effect might this have on their ministry? Keeping the purpose in mind will guide your thinking, planning, and leading.

3. Plan Your Approach

Think about the outline you will follow in the discussion. Specifically, think about how you will introduce the case, how you will make the transition to the main discussion and how that discussion will be structured, and how you will conclude the case.

The introduction should be brief and can take the form of a statement, a question, picking up a phrase or statement in the case, or providing a summary of the case. Focusing on the time line may be helpful if the sequence of events is important. Asking someone to give a two-minute summary of the case might be a good way to start, focusing the group's collective attention on the details of the case.

In the introduction, identify key issues so the group will know what the focus will be. Key issues can be stated by the teacher or can be solicited ideas from the group.

In long cases, such as those in this book, group members should read the case prior to coming together for discussion. Otherwise too much group time is taken reading the case. Shorter cases can be read silently at the beginning of the meeting, especially if the leader wants an element of surprise or immediate reaction to the issue at hand. When the case is read ahead of time, an oral summary at the start of discussion is essential.

Plan ahead how to transition from the introduction to the main discussion. One effective transition is to ask group members to recall significant information about the central characters in the case. Jot this information on a chalkboard or overhead projector and ask if anyone wants to comment on any particular piece of information. This helps group members recall names and information about specific people in the case.

Following some discussion on the characters, ask what issues group members noted in their reading. Write this information on the board or overhead as well, and state or ask what issues need to be discussed. Let this form the structure for the primary discussion time with the group.

Some case teachers prefer to break a large group into smaller clusters of three to five people to discuss particular aspects of a case. In this method, it is best to have the clusters discuss different issues with some method of reporting their findings back to the whole group. Then the leader needs to finalize the discussion with everyone reconvened, pulling any loose strands together and summarizing the findings into a coherent whole.

Another approach, which I prefer, is to keep the whole group together with you as facilitator. This can be done even in large groups. It allows everyone to hear what others say and keeps the group moving together. Even though unanimity may not be achieved, nor is it necessarily the goal, keeping the group together does mean the group thinks together and may reach deeper understanding of the issues than is possible when the group is broken into smaller clusters.

Another effective method is the use of role play. Individuals take on the roles of specific characters in the case, and based on the information in the case, they talk to each other in that role. This heightens the drama and makes the issues real for the individuals participating in the role play as well as for the observers, but it must be done well to be effective. Some people are uncomfortable role-playing, so either select individuals you know will do a good job or let individuals volunteer.

For the conclusion, it is not necessary to have everything neatly wrapped up. People may reach different conclusions on what they think needs to happen in a particular case. The goal is to get individuals to think about specific issues that will help them in their personal growth and ministry, not to get everyone to agree on a particular issue. Often a member of the group will continue to reflect on the discussion long after the time together, and the result may be further growth and change.

But the discussion does need closure. That can come from a summary of what has been said, a reiteration of the issues and possible resolutions, a challenge to learn from the case in some specific way, speculation on what may have eventually happened in the case, or raising a question for participants to further reflect on individually. Citing biblical references for people to think about or praying for each other in relation to the issues portrayed in the case are further effective ways to draw the discussion to a close.

4. Guide the Discussion

The leader's task is to guide the discussion to maximize learning for the group. This needs to be done without manipulating the group for one's own agenda, although the leader may have a particular point of view that can be expressed for the group to consider. Sometimes a "minilecture" is effective, particularly on an issue of the leader's expertise, but it may be best to allow the group to deal with the issues in a discussion format.

Raise questions and allow people time to think about their responses. Don't ask several questions at once on different aspects of an issue. That hinders the group from focusing on something in depth. Use questions to focus attention on the topic, and avoid going several directions at once.

Sometimes an individual will raise a question or make a comment about an issue that deserves discussion but interrupts the flow of discussion on a particular point. When this happens, the leader can jot down the point on the overhead or chalkboard and say the point will be discussed later. Then steer the discussion back to the question at hand.

If someone expresses an opinion that you sense may not be held by others, ask the group to respond. Or if you know the group members well, you may request a specific individual to respond. You want to facilitate the group's dealing with the issues, not always respond yourself to each comment or question raised by others.

Sometimes a group will have members who are quiet and need to be invited to make comments. Often these quieter members have keen insights, so a good leader will find appropriate ways to include such people in the discussion without being too obvious or intrusive.

Keep an eye on the clock. Ninety minutes is the maximum time most adults are at their best in thinking and interacting in a group situation. The cases in this book can be discussed effectively in one hour or less. The better your planning in advance, the more effective will be your use of time.

5. Use Visuals When Possible

Case teaching provides a forum that maximizes group interaction. Although a discussion with no use of visuals can be productive, good visuals enhance the outcome and learning. This may be nothing more than the use of an overhead projector or chalkboard to jot down major points or plot out a time line. It could also be the use of prepared transparencies to be used with an overhead to organize the themes of a case.

Use of newsprint with bold markers is a tried-and-true method of listing significant points in a discussion. But use your imagination. There are many ways to introduce something visual to engage participants and enhance learning.

6. Obtain Feedback for Evaluation

You will want to obtain information to help in evaluating what worked and what did not work in teaching a case as well as help in understanding your approach and style in leading the discussion. You can solicit such feedback from the group as a whole on occasion, or request it from individuals in a private conversation. Another good way to obtain helpful information is by having a colleague join the group to evaluate your group leadership using an interaction chart (a graph showing the location of people in the group, who spoke to whom, and how many times an individual spoke).

The more experience you have teaching cases, the more you gain confidence and new ideas in using cases. Everyone involved may discover anew the value of a group discussing an issue of importance. Focusing on real situations forces us to deal with reality.

Case teaching is not the only way to learn, of course. Nor does it fit every learning need. But it can be a powerful way of helping group members deal with issues in their own lives that might otherwise be ignored. Case stories are often our own stories, or we can to some extent identify with specific items in a case. Judicious use of cases, either for personal reading and reflection or for group discussion, can be used of God to bring about clarity of thought and facilitate needed change in behavior.

Let me repeat what I stated in the introduction: Good case teaching will make good use of biblical material. The use of cases is not intended to provide an opportunity just to exchange human wisdom, but more so to wrestle with biblical teaching and how it applies to the dilemmas of real people—in this book, pastors.

Although we must make use of the rich resource of support available to us through colleagues in ministry who will love us, challenge us, pray for us, and walk with us in the various crises we face in our own lives, nothing will substitute for a thorough knowledge of Scripture, a personal zeal for holiness in Christ, and a rigorous application of biblical truth to our lives. Good discussion using the case method will keep this reality paramount.

Suggested Reading

Anger

Books

Augsburger, David W. *Anger and Assertiveness in Pastoral Care.* Philadelphia: Fortress, 1979.

Hauck, Paul A. *Overcoming Frustration and Anger.* Philadelphia: Westminster, 1974.

Tavris, Carol. *Anger: The Misunderstood Emotion.* New York: Simon and Schuster, 1982.

Walters, Richard P. *Anger: Yours and Mine and What to Do about It.* Grand Rapids: Zondervan, 1981.

Warren, Neil Clark. *Make Anger Your Ally.* Garden City, N.H.: Doubleday, 1985.

Call

Books

Clifford, Paul Rowntree. *The Pastoral Calling.* Great Neck, N.Y.: Channel, 1961.

Gillaspie, Gerald Whiteman. *The Restless Pastor.* Chicago: Moody, 1974.

Green, Michael. *Called to Serve.* Grand Rapids: Baker, 1981.

Paul, Cecil R. *Passages of a Pastor*. Grand Rapids: Zondervan, 1981.

Sanford, John A. *Ministry Burnout*. New York: Paulist, 1982.

Articles

Brown, Alistair. "When You Feel Empty." *Leadership* 11, no. 3 (Summer 1990): 118–22.

Kesler, Jay. "Why We Love and Hate Ministry." *Leadership* 11, no. 2 (Spring 1990): 84–89.

Patterson, Ben, et. al. "The Call: Is Ministry a Career?" *Leadership* 11, no. 3 (Summer 1990): 52–61.

Patterson, LeRoy. "Do I Belong in the Ministry?" *Leadership* 6, no. 1 (Winter 1985): 79–81.

Quick, Kenneth B. "Pastors and the Peter Principle." *Leadership* 11, no. 3 (Summer 1990): 100–105.

Candidating

Books

Brister, C. W., James L. Cooper, and J. David Fite. *Beginning Your Ministry*. Nashville: Abingdon, 1981.

Gallaspie, Gerald Whiteman. *The Restless Pastor*. Chicago: Moody, 1974.

Hahn, Celia A. *The Minister Is Leaving*. New York: Seabury, 1974.

Harris, John C. *The Minister Looks for a Job*. Washington: Alban Institute, 1977.

Kemper, Robert G. *Beginning a New Pastorate*. Nashville: Abingdon, 1978.

Articles

Berkley, Jim. "Have I Come to the Wrong Church?" *Leadership* 7, no. 2 (Spring 1986): 50–57.

———. "The Unfinished Pastor." *Leadership* 5, no. 4 (Fall 1984): 128–29.

Bird, Warren. "Aids for Selecting the New Pastor." *Leadership* 3, no. 2 (Spring 1982): 100–101.

Chapman, Mrs. Floyd, and Stephen Englehardt. "Suggestions

for an Effective First Pastorate." *Leadership* 1, no. 3 (Summer 1980): 63–64.

Coughlin, Michael F. "Full-Time Pastor, Part-Time Pay." *Leadership* 12, no. 2 (Spring 1991): 111–13.

Griffin, Em. "Confessions of a Pulpit Committee." *Leadership* 4, no. 4 (Fall 1983): 106–113.

Holck, Manfred, Jr. "Parsonage or Housing Allowance—Which Is Better?" *Leadership* 1, no. 2 (Spring 1980): 54–58.

Osborne, Larry W. "Negotiating a Fair Salary." *Leadership* 8, no. 1 (Winter 1987): 84–88.

Patterson, Ben. "The Wilderness of the Candidate." *Leadership* 4, no. 4 (Fall 1983): 20–23.

Pearson, John. "How to Create an Employment Agreement." *Leadership* 1, no. 2 (Spring 1980): 91–94.

Quick, Kenneth B. "Candid Candidating." *Leadership* 11, no. 4 (Fall 1990): 70–75.

Rumford, Douglas J. "The Art of the Start." *Leadership* 10, no. 2 (Spring 1989): 82–87.

———. "Starting Out and Staying In." *Leadership* 4, no. 2 (Spring 1983): 94–96.

Scott, Douglas G. "Getting the Real Story: A Guide to Candidating." *Leadership* 5, no. 3 (Summer 1984): 24–29.

Senter, Mark H., III. "Five Stages in Your Ministry Development." *Leadership* 10, no. 2 (Spring 1989): 88–96.

Wilkerson, Dave. "The Square Pastor in a Round Church." *Leadership* 11, no. 1 (Winter 1990): 84–88.

Wilson, Everett L. "Pastoring Begins with the Search Committee." *Leadership* 11, no. 4 (Fall 1990): 74–75.

Conflict

Books

Berkley, James D. *Called into Crisis*. Waco: Leadership/Word, 1989.

Buzzard, Lynn, and Laurence Eck. *Tell It to the Church: Reconciling out of Court*. Elgin, IL: David C. Cook, 1982.

Fairfield, James G. T. *When You Don't Agree*. Scottdale, Pa.: Herald Press, 1977.

Halverstadt, Hugh F. *Managing Church Conflict*. Louisville: Westminster/John Knox, 1991.

Huttenlocker, Keith. *Conflict and Caring: Preventing, Managing, and Resolving Conflict in the Church*. Grand Rapids: Zondervan, 1988.

Kittlaus, Paul, and Speed Leas. *Church Fights*. Philadelphia: Westminster, 1973.

Kraybill, Ronald S. *Repairing the Breach: Ministering in Community Conflict*. Scottdale, Pa.: Herald Press, 1981.

Leas, Speed B. *Leadership and Conflict*. Nashville: Abingdon, 1982.

LeFevre, Perry D., ed. *Conflict in a Voluntary Association*. Chicago: Exploration Press, 1975.

Lewis, Douglass. *Resolving Church Conflicts*. San Francisco: Harper and Row, 1981.

McDonough, Reginald M. *Working with Volunteer Leaders in the Church*. Nashville: Broadman, 1976.

McSwain, Larry, and William C. Treadwell, Jr. *Conflict Ministry in the Church*. Nashville: Broadman, 1980.

Miller, John M. *The Contentious Community*. Philadelphia: Westminster, 1978.

Pneuman, Roy W., and Margaret E. Bruehl. *Managing Conflict: A Complete Process-Centered Handbook*. Englewood Cliffs, N.J.: Prentice-Hall, 1982.

Prinzing, Fred W. *Handling Church Tensions Creatively*. Arlington Heights, Ill.: Harvest Publications, 1986.

Schaller, Lyle E. *Activating the Passive Church*. Nashville: Abingdon, 1981.

———. *Effective Church Planning*. Nashville: Abingdon, 1979.

———. *Survival Tactics in the Parish*. Nashville: Abingdon, 1977.

Articles

Berkley, James D. "Damage Control for Mistakes." *Leadership* 8, no. 3 (Spring 1987): 54–60.

Bubna, Don. "Ten Reasons Not to Resign." *Leadership* 4, no. 4 (Fall 1983): 74–80.

Burnham, Monty, et. al. "Leadership Forum. Conflict: Facing It in Yourself and in Your Church." *Leadership* 1, no. 2 (Spring 1980): 23–36.

Buzzard, Lynn. "War and Peace in the Local Church." *Leadership* 4, no. 3 (Summer 1983): 20–30.

Cerling, Charles, Jr. "Getting Fired: A Testimony." *Leadership* 6, no. 1 (Winter 1985): 88–93.

Cionca, John R. "To Fight or Not to Fight." *Leadership* 6, no. 2 (Spring 1985): 86–89.

Crowell, Rodney. "Spiritual Survival for a Forced Exit." *Leadership* 10, no. 1 (Winter 1989): 26–30.

Gonzales, Gary, et. al. "Anatomy of a Church Fight." *Leadership* 4, no. 3 (Summer 1983): 96–103.

Hall, Robert K. "A Strategy for Facing Difficult People." *Leadership* 6, no. 1 (Winter 1985): 58–59.

Kraybill, Ronald S. "Handling Holy Wars." *Leadership* 7, no. 4 (Fall 1986): 30–38.

Leas, Speed. "Inside Church Fights" (interview). *Leadership* 9, no. 1 (Winter 1989): 12–20.

———. "Rooting out Causes of Conflict." *Leadership* 13, no. 2 (Spring 1992): 54–61.

Mains, David. "My Greatest Ministry Mistakes" (interview). *Leadership* 1, no. 2 (Spring 1980): 15–22.

Merrill, Dean. "After the Fiasco: Restoring Fallen Christians." *Leadership* 4, no. 4 (Fall 1983): 58–63.

Moeller, Robert L. "Pastor David or Pastor Solomon?" *Leadership* 10, no. 1 (Winter 1989): 104–109.

Newbold, Robert T., Jr. "Conflict in the Black Church." *Leadership* 1, no. 2 (Spring 1980): 99–101.

Osborne, Larry W. "Removing Roadblocks to Board Unity." *Leadership* 7, no. 4 (Fall 1986): 84–89.

Patterson, Ben. "A Small Pump at the Edge of the Swamp?" *Leadership* 1, no. 2 (Spring 1980): 41–46.

Porter, Richard. "Piecing Together a Shattered Church." *Leadership* 9, no. 2 (Spring 1988): 83–89.

Price, Roy C. "Building Trust between Pastor and Congregation." *Leadership* 1, no. 2 (Spring 1980): 47–53.

————. "When the Pastor Gets Fired." *Leadership* 4, no. 4 (Fall 1983): 50–55.

Ratz, Calvin C. "The Loneliest Choice of All." *Leadership* 6, no. 1 (Winter 1985): 74–78.

Rottenberg, Isaac. "Christian versus Christian." *Leadership* 1, no. 2 (Spring 1980): 59–64.

Shelley, Marshall. "Surviving a Power Play." *Leadership* 6, no. 1 (Winter 1985): 50–57.

Spickelmier, Jim. "Spittin' Out Peas: When the Question Is Control." *Leadership* 10, no. 2 (Spring 1989): 118–22.

Swindoll, Charles R. "Toward Better Board Relationships." *Leadership* 7, no. 4 (Fall 1986): 90–93.

Wetherwax, John R. "Holding Your Ground." *Leadership* 9, no. 2 (Spring 1988): 114–18.

Wise, Robert L. "When Mindsets Collide." *Leadership* 7, no. 4 (Fall 1986): 22–28.

————. "Wounded Warriors in the Woods." *Leadership* 6, no. 4 (Fall 1985): 56–60.

Congregational Support
Books

Enroth, Ronald M. *Churches That Abuse*. Grand Rapids: Zondervan, 1992.

Willimon, William H. *Clergy and Laity Burnout*. Nashville: Abingdon, 1989.

Articles

Boers, Arthur. "Everyone's Pastor; No One's Friend." *Leadership* 12, no. 1 (Winter 1991): 130–34.

Harris, Steve. "Helping People Help You." *Leadership* 9, no. 1 (Winter 1988): 98–102.

————. "When the Pastor Is Hurting." *Leadership* 6, no. 2 (Spring 1985): 108–13.

Larson, Bruce. "Caring for the Congregation's Caregivers." *Leadership* 12, no. 1 (Winter 1991): 124.

Olsen, David C., and William Grosch. "Clergy Burnout: A Self Psychology and Systems Perspective." *Journal of Pastoral Care* 45, no. 3 (Fall 1991): 297–304.

Cross-Cultural Ministry
Articles

Groh, Lucille Sider, et. al. "Counseling Hispanics in the United States." *Journal of Pastoral Care* 44, no. 1 (Spring 1990): 33–41.

Johanson, Gregory J. "A Critical Analysis of Pastoral Counseling Across Cultures." *Journal of Pastoral Counseling* 46, no. 2 (Summer 1992): 162–73.

Klassen, Ron. "Retooling for Rural Ministry." *Leadership* 10, no. 3 (Spring 1989): 82–87.

Silva-Netto, Benoni. "Pastoral Counseling in a Multicultural Context." *Journal of Pastoral Care* 46, no. 2 (Summer 1992): 131–39.

Depression
Books

Baker, Don, and Emery Nester. *Depression: Finding Hope and Meaning in Life's Darkest Shadow.* Portland, Oreg.: Multnomah, 1983.

Beck, Aaron T. *Depression: Cause and Treatment.* Philadelphia: University of Pennsylvania Press, 1987.

Gaddy, C. Welton. *A Soul under Siege: Surviving Clergy Depression.* Philadelphia: Westminster/John Knox, 1991.

Hart, Archibald D. *Coping with Depression in the Ministry and Other Helping Professions.* Waco: Word, 1984.

Hauck, Paul A. *Overcoming Depression.* Philadelphia: Westminster, 1973.

White, John. *The Masks of Melancholy: A Christian Physician Looks at Depression and Suicide.* Downers Grove, Ill.: InterVarsity Press, 1982.

Articles

Bustanoby, Andre. "Finding Hope in Failure." *Leadership* 8, no. 2 (Spring 1987): 30–31.

Currie, Susan and David. "Escaping the Swamp of Depression." *Leadership* 13, no. 1 (Winter 1992): 100–105.

Hughes, R. Kent. "Feelings of Failure." *Leadership* 8, no. 2 (Spring 1987): 22–29.

Martin, Enos D. "Depression in the Clergy." *Leadership* 3, no. 1 (Winter 1982): 81–89.

Miller, Kevin A. "The Exacting Price of Ministry." *Leadership* 8, no. 2 (Spring 1987): 38–46.

Vanderwell, Howard D. "Turning Weakness into Strength." *Leadership* 7, no. 3 (Summer 1986): 122–27.

Determining the Leading of God

Books

Friesen, Garry. *Decision Making and the Will of God.* Portland: Multnomah, 1980.

Harbaugh, Gary L. *Pastor as Person: Maintaining Personal Integrity in the Choices and Challenges of Ministry.* Minneapolis: Augsburg, 1984.

Smith, M. Blaine. *Knowing God's Will: Biblical Principles of Guidance.* Downers Grove, Ill.: InterVarsity, 1979.

Discouragement

Books

Carlson, Dwight L. *Run and Not Be Weary.* Old Tappan, N.J.: Revell, 1974.

Zeluff, Daniel. *There's Algae in the Baptismal "Fount."* Nashville: Abingdon, 1978.

Articles

Chambers, Oswald. "Where Do You Look for Encouragement?" *Leadership* 7, no. 3 (Spring 1986): 33–35.

Gonzales, Gary. "Honest Praise: A Pastor's Emotional Fuel." *Leadership* 3, no. 4 (Fall 1982): 49–53.

Guernsey, Dennis B. "Family and Church: Who Supports Whom?" *Leadership* 7, no. 1 (Winter 1986): 77–79.

Family Background Affecting Current Behavior
Books

McBurney, Louis. *Counseling Christian Workers.* Waco: Word, 1986.

Missildine, W. Hugh. *Your Inner Child of the Past.* New York: Simon and Schuster, 1963.

Osborne, Cicil. *The Art of Understanding Yourself.* Grand Rapids: Zondervan, 1967.

Articles

Berkley, James D. "Making Use of Your Past." *Leadership* 6, no. 3 (Summer 1985): 108–13.

Family Problems of the Pastor
Books

Bailey, Robert W. *Coping with Stress in the Minister's Home.* Nashville: Broadman, 1979.

Balswick, Jack O., and Judith K. Balswick. *The Family: A Christian Perspective on the Contemporary Home.* Grand Rapids: Baker, 1991.

Bouma, Gary, and Mary LaGrand Bouma. *Divorce in the Parsonage.* Minneapolis: Bethany Fellowship, 1979.

Campbell, Dennis M. *The Yoke of Obedience.* Nashville: Abingdon, 1988.

Garsee, Jarrell W. *What You Always Wanted to Know about Your Pastor-Husband.* Kansas City: Beacon Hill Press, 1978.

Lee, Cameron. *PK: Helping Pastors' Kids through Their Identity Crisis.* Grand Rapids: Zondervan, 1992.

Lee, Cameron, and Jack Balswick. *Life in a Glass House.* Grand Rapids: Zondervan, 1989.

Mace, David R. and Vera. *What's Happening to Clergy Marriages?* Nashville: Abingdon, 1980.

Madsden, Keith. *Fallen Images: Experiencing Divorce in the Ministry.* Valley Forge, Pa.: Judson, 1985.

Mickey, Paul A., and Ginny W. Ashmore. *Clergy Families: Is Normal Life Possible?* Grand Rapids: Zondervan, 1991.

Minirth, Frank, ed. *The Workaholic and His Family.* Grand Rapids: Baker, 1981.

Nordland, Frances. *The Unprivate Life of the Pastor's Wife.* Chicago: Moody, 1972.

Oswald, Roy M. *Married to the Minister.* Washington, D.C.: Alban Institute, 1980.

Sinclair, Donna. *The Pastor's Wife Today.* Nashville: Abingdon, 1981.

Articles

Baker, David C., and Jean Pearson Scott. "Predictors of Well-Being among Pastors' Wives: A Comparison with Nonclergy Wives." *Journal of Pastoral Care* 46, no. 1 (Spring 1992): 33–43.

Bouma, Mary, et. al. "Leadership Forum: When the Ministerial Family Caves In." *Leadership* 4, no. 2 (Spring 1983): 97–113.

Bouma, Mary LaGrand. "Ministers' Wives: The Walking Wounded." *Leadership* 1, no. 1 (Winter 1980): 63–75.

Lee, Milton. "Pastoring with Hurts at Home." *Leadership* 10, no. 2 (Spring 1989): 98–105.

Rice, Bonnie Shipley. "Married to the Man in the Ministry." *Leadership* 12, no. 1 (Winter 1991): 68–73.

Valeriano, Pat. "A Survey of Ministers' Wives." *Leadership* 2, no. 4 (Fall 1981): 64–73.

Financial Stress

Books

Barrett, Wayne C. *Clergy Personal Finance.* Nashville: Abingdon, 1990.

Holck, Manfred, Jr. *Making It on a Pastor's Pay.* Nashville: Abingdon, 1974.

————. *The Minister's Handbook for Personal Finance.* Minneapolis: Augsburg, 1990.

Meyer, Kenneth M. *Minister's Guide to Financial Planning.* Grand Rapids: Zondervan, 1987.

Articles

Allaby, Stan, et. al. "Leadership Forum: Financial Facts of Pastoral Life." *Leadership* 8, no. 1 (Winter 1987): 130–37.

Bergstrom, Richard L. "Stunned by an Inside Job." *Leadership* 8, no. 1 (Winter 1987): 102–10.

Hayner, Jerry. "The Uneasy Marriage of Money and Ministry" (interview). *Leadership* 8, no. 1 (Winter 1987): 12–19.

Muck, Terry. "Dangerous Decisions." *Leadership* 8, no. 1 (Winter 1987): 46–52.

White, Charles Edward. "What Wesley Practiced and Preached about Money." *Leadership* 8, no. 1 (Winter 1987): 27–29.

Male-Female Gender Issues

Books

Eldridge, O. John. *Women Pastors: If God Calls, Why Not the Church?* Valley Forge, Pa.: Judson, 1981.

Marie, Anne. *The Male-Female Church Staff.* Washington, D.C.: The Alban Institute, 1990.

Schaper, Donna. *Common Sense about Men and Women in Ministry.* Washington, D.C.: The Alban Institute, 1990.

Tannen, Deborah. *You Just Don't Understand: Women and Men in Conversation.* New York: Ballantine Books, 1990.

Articles

Bly, Stephen. "Molding Ministry to Fit Men." *Leadership* 12, no. 1 (Winter, 1991): 52–57.

Bustanoby, Andre. "Counseling the Seductive Female." *Leadership* 9, no. 1 (Winter 1988): 48–54.

Gaede-Penner, Naomi. "Ministries among Today's Women." *Leadership* 12, no. 1 (Winter 1991): 58–62.

Galli, Mark. "What Do Men Want?" *Leadership* 12, no. 1 (Winter 1991): 36–44.

Miller, Mary, Alice Peterson, and Jim Smith. "How Gender Specific Is Ministry?" (forum). *Leadership* 12, no. 1 (Winter 1991): 24–35.

Phillips, Michael E. "Appropriate Affection." *Leadership* 9, no. 1 (Winter 1988): 108–12.

Schwartz, Richard S. "A Psychiatrist's View of Transference and Countertransference in the Pastoral Relationship." *Journal of Pastoral Care* 43, no. 1 (Spring 1989): 41–46.

Sexual Misbehavior

Books

Alsdurf, James, and Phyllis Alsdurf. *Battered into Submission: The Tragedy of Wife Abuse in the Christian Home.* Downers Grove, Ill.: InterVarsity Press, 1989.

Baker, Don. *Beyond Forgiveness.* Waco: Word, 1986.

Blair, Charles. *The Man Who Could Do No Wrong.* Lincoln, Va.: Chosen, 1981.

Bonhoeffer, Dietrich. *Creation and Fall/Temptation.* New York: Macmillan, 1965.

Feldmeth, Joanne Ross, and Midge Wallace Finley. *We Weep for Ourselves and Our Children: A Christian Guide for Survivors of Childhood Sexual Abuse.* San Francisco: Harper, 1990.

Fortune, Marie M. *Is Nothing Sacred? When Sex Invades the Pastoral Relationship.* San Francisco: Harper, 1989.

Heggen, Carolyn Holderread. *Sexual Abuse in Christian Homes and Churches.* Scottdale, Pa.: Herald Press, 1993.

Lavender, Lucille. *They Cry Too.* Wheaton: Tyndale, 1979.

Lebacqz, Karen, and Ronald G. Barton. *Sex in the Parish.* Louisville: Westminster/John Knox, 1991.

McBurney, Louis. *Counseling Christian Workers.* Waco: Word, 1986.

Merrill, Dean. *Another Chance.* Grand Rapids: Zondervan, 1981.

Oates, Wayne E. *The Minister's Own Mental Health.* Great Neck, N.Y.: Channel, 1955.

Penner, Clifford and Joyce. *The Gift of Sex.* Dallas: Word, 1981.

Rassieur, Charles L. *The Problem Clergymen Don't Talk About.* Philadelphia: Westminster, 1976.

Rutter, Peter. *Sex in the Forbidden Zone: When Men in Power— Therapists, Doctors, Clergy, Teachers and Others—Betray Women's Trust.* Los Angeles: J. P. Tarcher, 1989.

Schaumburg, Harry. *False Intimacy: Understanding the Struggle of Sexual Addiction.* Colorado Springs: NavPress, 1992.

Trobisch, Walter. *Living with Unfulfilled Desires.* Downers Grove, Ill.: InterVarsity Press, 1976.

Trobisch, Walter and Ingrid. *My Beautiful Feeling.* Downers Grove, Ill.: InterVarsity, 1976.

White, John. *Eros Defiled.* Downers Grove, Ill.: InterVarsity, 1977.

Wilson, Earl D. *Sexual Sanity: Breaking Free from Uncontrolled Habits.* Downers Grove, Ill.: InterVarsity Press, 1984.

Articles

Alcorn, Randy. "Strategies to Keep from Falling." *Leadership* 9, no. 1 (Winter 1988): 42–47.

Bryce, Heather. "After the Affair: A Wife's Story." *Leadership* 9, no. 1 (Winter 1988): 58–65.

Dobson, Edward G. "Restoring a Fallen Colleague." *Leadership* 13, no. 1 (Winter 1992): 106–21.

Editors. "How Common Is Pastoral Indiscretion?" *Leadership* 9, no. 1 (Winter 1988): 12–13.

Frey, William, et. al. "Forum: Creating a Restoration Process." *Leadership* 13, no. 1 (Winter 1992): 122–34.

Hart, Arch, et. al. "Leadership Forum: Private Sins of Public Ministry." *Leadership* 9, no. 1 (Winter 1988): 14–23.

Hart, Archibald. "Transference: Loosening the Tie That Binds." *Leadership* 3, no. 4 (Fall 1982): 110–17.

Hybels, Bill. "Preaching on the Oh-So-Delicate Subject." *Leadership* 9, no. 1 (Winter 1988): 120–26.

McBurney, Louis. "Avoiding the Scarlet Letter." *Leadership* 6, no. 3 (Summer 1985): 44–51.

McBurney, Louis. "Treatment for Infidelity Fallout." *Leadership* 7, no. 2 (Spring 1986): 112–19.

Name Withheld. "The War Within." *Leadership* 3, no. 4 (Fall 1982): 30–48.

Name Withheld. "The War within Continues." *Leadership* 9, no. 1 (Winter 1988): 24–33.

Name Withheld. "When a Pastoral Colleague Falls." *Leadership* 12, no. 1 (Winter 1991): 102–11.

Sandholm, Gayle L. "The Changing Face of Marriage and Extramarital Relationships." *Journal of Pastoral Care* 43, no. 3 (Fall 1989): 249–58.

Willoughby, Kathryn. "The Sex Issue: Four Women Respond." *Leadership* 9, no. 3 (Summer 1988): 57–59.

Spiritual Life of Pastor

Books

McKenna, David L. *Renewing Our Ministry*. Waco: Word, 1986.

Moreman, William M. *Developing Spiritually and Professionally*. Philadelphia: Westminster, 1984.

Packer, J. I. *A Quest for Godliness*. Wheaton, Ill.: Crossway Books, 1990.

Peterson, Eugene H. *The Contemplative Pastor*. Waco: Leadership/ Word, 1989.

Sanders, J. Oswald. *Spiritual Leadership*. Chicago: Moody, 1967.

Willard, Dallas. *The Spirit of the Disciplines: Understanding How God Changes Lives*. San Francisco: Harper, 1988.

Articles

Littleton, Mark R. "Some Quiet Confessions about Quiet Time." *Leadership* 4, no. 4 (Fall 1983): 81–85.

McBurney, Louis. "A Psychiatrist Looks at Troubled Pastors." *Leadership* 1, no. 2 (Spring 1980): 107–20.

McKenna, David L. "Recycling Pastors." *Leadership* 1, no. 4 (Fall 1980): 24–30.

Muck, Terry. "Ten Questions about the Devotional Life." *Leadership* 3, no. 1 (Winter 1982): 30–39.

Myra, Harold L. "Oswald Chambers: Insights to Deepen Your Ministry." *Leadership* 3, no. 1 (Winter 1982): 47–58.

Peterson, Eugene H. "Growth: An Act of the Will?" *Leadership* 9, no. 4 (Fall 1988): 34–40.

———. "Recovering Passion for God." *Leadership* 11, no. 1 (Winter 1990): 64–71.

———. "The Unbusy Pastor." *Leadership* 2, no. 3 (Summer 1981): 70–76.

Sanny, Lorne C. "How to Spend a Day in Prwyer." *Leadership* 3, no. 3 (Summer 1982): 71–75.

Thielicke, Helmut. "Talking about God or with God?" *Leadership* 1, no. 3 (Summer 1980): 48–56.

Walrath, Douglas Alan. "When Spirituality Is Just a Job." *Leadership* 9, no. 4 (Fall 1988): 62–63.

Wayman, Dennis L. "A Spiritual-Life Checkup." *Leadership* 4, no. 4 (Fall 1983): 88–89.

Staff Relationships

Books

Schaller, Lyle E. *The Multiple Staff and the Larger Church.* Nashville: Abingdon, 1980.

———. *The Senior Minister.* Nashville: Abingdon, 1988.

Articles

Berkley, James. "How Pastors and Associates Get Along." *Leadership* 7, no. 1 (Winter 1986): 108–12.

Borthwick, Paul. "To Fire or Not to Fire." *Leadership* 6, no. 1 (Winter 1985): 82–87.

Bradford, Robert C. "Growing Your Own Staff." *Leadership* 5, no. 2 (Spring 1984): 84–88.

Ceynar, Marvin. "A Survival Kit for Associate Pastors." *Leadership* 3, no. 1 (Winter 1982): 38–39.

Epps, David. "'Just' an Associate Pastor." *Leadership* 2, no. 1 (Winter 1981): 120–21.

Galli, Mark. "Awakening from an Assistant Pastorate." *Leadership* 7, no. 1 (Winter 1986): 113–15.

Gerig, Don, et. al. "Leadership Forum: Who Needs a Staff?" *Leadership* 6, no. 3 (Summer 1985): 126–36.

Hunter, Kent R. "A Model for Multiple Staff Management." *Leadership* 2, no. 3 (Summer 1981): 99–107.

Jacobsen, Wayne L. "Caught in the Middle." *Leadership* 1, no. 2 (Spring 1980): 83–90.

———. "Seven Reasons for Staff Conflict." *Leadership* 4, no. 3 (Summer 1983): 34–39.

Kageler, Len. "Performance Reviews: Worth the Trouble?" *Leadership* 6, no. 3 (Summer 1985): 24–28.

Martin, Gilbert R., with Daniel W. Pawley. "Testing Staff Relationships in the High Sierras." *Leadership* 2, no. 2 (Spring 1981): 79–86.

Miller, Calvin. "Fiddlin' with the Staff." *Leadership* 7, no. 1 (Winter 1986): 105–7.

Muck, Terry. "How I Motivate My Staff." *Leadership* 1, no. 3 (Summer 1980): 81–84.

Osten, Donald C. "Ambition and the Assistant Pastor." *Leadership* 3, no. 4 (Fall 1982): 52–53.

Shawchuck, Norman. "A Candid Letter to Senior Pastors." *Leadership* 1, no. 3 (Summer 1980): 85–87.

Smith, Chris. "Sweet Music from a Second Fiddle." *Leadership* 11, no. 4 (Fall 1990): 66–68.

Smith, Fred. "Building the Church Staff." *Leadership* 3, no. 4 (Fall 1982): 99–104.

Sterrenburg, Sharon. "What Makes a Staff Succeed?" *Leadership* 11, no. 4 (Fall 1990): 69.

Stress

Books

Ecker, Richard E. *The Stress Myth.* Downers Grove, Ill.: InterVarsity Press, 1985.

Harris, John C. *Stress, Power, and Ministry.* Washington, D. C.: The Alban Institute, 1977.

Hart, Archibald T. *Adrenalin and Stress.* Waco: Word, 1986.

Hulme, William E. *Managing Stress in Ministry.* San Francisco: Harper, 1985.

Rassieur, Charles L. *Christian Renewal: Living beyond Burnout.* Philadelphia: Westminster, 1984.

———. *Stress Management for Ministers.* Philadelphia: Westminster, 1982.

Sanford, John A. *Ministry Burnout.* Louisville: Westminster/John Knox, 1982.

Sehnert, Keith W. *Stress/Unstress.* Minneapolis: Augsburg, 1981.

Selye, Hans. *Stress without Distress.* New York: Lippincott-Signet, 1975.

———. *The Stress of Life.* New York: McGraw-Hill, 1976.

Articles

Gerig, Donald. "Are We Overworked?" *Leadership* 7, no. 3 (Summer 1986): 22–25.

Malony, H. Newton, with Donald Falkenberg. "Ministerial Burnout." *Leadership* 1, no. 4 (Fall 1980): 71–74.

"Ministry-Related Stress" (survey). *Leadership* 5, no. 1 (Winter 1984): 95–96.

Musholt, Daniel Martin. "Stress Management and Contemplative Spirituality." *Journal of Pastoral Care* 43, no. 2 (Summer 1989): 121–28.

Wald, Jack and Ann. "The Facts and Feelings of Overwork." *Leadership* 4, no. 2 (Spring 1983): 85–89.

Worship and Music

Books

Allen, Ronald, and Gordon Borror. *Worship: Rediscovering the Missing Jewel.* Portland: Multnomah, 1982.

Berkley, James D., gen. ed. *Leadership Handbooks of Practical Theology.*,Vol. 1. See Part 1, "Word and Worship," and Part III,"Music." Grand Rapids: Baker, 1992.

Engle, Paul E. *Discovering the Fullness of Worship.* Philadelphia: Great Commission, 1978.

Liesch, Barry. *People in the Presence of God: Models and Directions for Worship.* Grand Rapids: Zondervan, 1988.

Suggested Reading

Martin, Ralph P. *The Worship of God: Some Theological, Pastoral, and Practical Reflections.* Grand Rapids: Eerdmans, 1982.

Thompson, Bard. *Liturgies of the Western Church.* Philadelphia: Fortress, 1961.

Webber, Robert E. *Evangelicals on the Canterbury Trail.* Waco: Word, 1985.

———. *Worship Is a Verb.* Waco: Word, 1985.

———. *Worship Old and New.* Grand Rapids: Zondervan, 1983.

Willimon, William H. *Preaching and Leading Worship.* Louisville: Westminster/John Knox, 1984.

Articles

Anderson, Paul. "Balancing Form and Freedom." *Leadership* 7, no. 2 (Spring 1986): 24–33.

Asimakoupoulos, Greg. "Are We Worshipping Yet?" *Leadership* 10, no. 3 (Summer 1989): 88–89.

Bisjak, Gilford. "Second Thoughts about a Second Service." *Leadership* 8, no. 4 (Fall 1987): 109–10.

Bolinder, Garth. "Closer Harmony with Church Musicians." *Leadership* 7, no. 2 (Spring 1986): 94–99.

Burchett, Dwight, and Steve Gardner. "Christian Music: The Cost Controversy." *Leadership* 11, no. 1 (Winter 1990): 102–8.

Huff, Ronn, Bruce Leafblad, Roger Pittelko, Bob Schmidgall, and Sherm Williams. "Worship: Preparing Yourself and Your Congregation" (forum). *Leadership* 2, no. 3 (Summer 1981): 113–22.

Killinger, John. "Preaching and Worship: The Essential Link" (interview). *Leadership* 7, no. 2 (Spring 1986): 122–30.

———. "Reviving the Rites of Worship." *Leadership* 10, no. 4 (Fall 1989): 82–86.

LeMon, Cal. "Surviving Sunday Morning Innovations." *Leadership* 7, no. 2 (Spring 1986): 84–90.

Patterson, Ben. "Can Worship Leaders Worship?" *Leadership* 7, no. 2 (Spring 1986): 34–38.

Pollock, Shirley. "Sunday Morning Worship Innovations." *Leadership* 3, no. 1 (Winter 1982): 101–104.